INTRODUCTION

Welcome to the world of digital publishing ~ the book you now hold in your hand, was printed using the latest state of the art digital technology. The advent of print-on-demand has forever changed the publishing process, never has information been so accessible and it is our hope that this book serves your informational needs for years to come. If this is your first exposure to digital publishing, we hope that you are pleased with the results. Many more titles of interest to the classic automobile and motorcycle enthusiast, collector and restorer are available via our website at www.VelocePress.com. We hope that you find this title as interesting as we do.

NOTE FROM THE PUBLISHER

The information presented is true and complete to the best of our knowledge. All recommendations are made without any guarantees on the part of the author or the publisher, who also disclaim all liability incurred with the use of this information.

TRADEMARKS

We recognize that some words, model names and designations, for example, mentioned herein are the property of the trademark holder. We use them for identification purposes only. This is not an official publication.

INFORMATION ON THE USE OF THIS PUBLICATION

This manual is an invaluable resource for those interested in performing their own maintenance. However, in today's information age we are constantly subject to changes in common practice, new technology, availability of improved materials and increased awareness of chemical toxicity. As such, it is advised that the user consult with an experienced professional prior to undertaking any procedure described herein. While every care has been taken to ensure correctness of information, it is obviously not possible to guarantee complete freedom from errors or omissions or to accept liability arising from such errors or omissions. Therefore, any individual that uses the information contained within, or elects to perform or participate in do-it-yourself repairs or modifications acknowledges that there is a risk factor involved and that the publisher or its associates cannot be held responsible for personal injury or property damage resulting from the use of the information or the outcome of such procedures.

WARNING!

One final word of advice, this publication is intended to be used as a reference guide, and when in doubt the reader should consult with a qualified technician.

PREFACE

RUDGE-WHITWORTH motor-cycles need no introduction to the public. For years past they have enjoyed a widespread popularity and have proved their road-worthiness and high performance in no uncertain manner by winning numerous important road races.

This handbook, while containing much valuable information for expert motor-cyclists, has been written to meet the special requirements of absolute novices also. Advice is given on how to get a machine on the road and how to avoid coming into unpleasant contact with the Law. Those who have no idea as to how the internal combustion engine works will find in Chapter III a detailed explanation written in simple language. Following this is a simple description of the Amal carburettor and Rudge ignition components.

Special attention is directed to Chapter IV, dealing with that vitally important matter, Lubrication. The Rudge lubrication system is as nearly perfect as is possible, but some responsibility naturally rests on the rider's shoulders, and neglect in this matter results in failure to obtain the best results and maximum life from a machine. The Rudge dry-sump lubrication system is clearly explained and a lubrication chart is included. The remainder of this book deals exhaustively with the garaging and maintenance of 1933-39 Rudge motor-cycles. Full instructions are given on how to make the various adjustments which are from time to time necessary, how to decarbonize and grind-in the valves, how to maintain the lighting and ignition system in perfect order, how to tune the carburettor, and how to strip down various components; and wiring diagrams will be found on pages 82 and 84.

Rudge motor-cycles are no longer manufactured, but owners of Rudges and prospective buyers of used Rudges should note that spare parts are obtainable from the following firms: Messrs. Kays

PREFACE

of Ealing, Ltd., 8–10 Bond Street, Ealing, London, W.5; Messrs. Godfreys, Ltd., 208 Great Portland Street, London, W.1.; Messrs. Claude Rye, Ltd., 895–921 Fulham Road, London, S.W.6; Messrs. Thomson's, 10 Cornmarket, Louth, Lincs; and Messrs. Alexanders, 48 City Road, Manchester. The last mentioned two firms, besides stocking a big variety of spare parts, also undertake engine, gearbox, and general overhauls. This also applies to Messrs. Godfreys, Ltd., who service Rudges of 1928–39 design. Note that although spares are obtainable from the address given above, all repair work by Messrs. Godfreys, Ltd., is dealt with at 7A Eden Street, Hampstead Road, London, N.W.1.

W. C. H.

FLOYD CLYMER'S MOTORCYCLIST'S LIBRARY

The Book of the
RUDGE

A COMPLETE GUIDE FOR OWNERS AND PROSPECTIVE PURCHASERS OF 1933–39 RUDGE-WHITWORTH MOTOR CYCLES

BY

L. H. CADE

AND

F. ANSTEY, B.Sc. (Eng.), A.M.I.A.E.

CHIEF DESIGNER, RUDGE-WHITWORTH, LTD.

REVISED BY

W. C. HAYCRAFT, F.R.S.A.

FIFTH EDITION

1953

ANNOUNCEMENT

By special arrangement with the original publishers of this book, Sir Isaac Pitman & Son, Ltd., of London, England, we have secured the exclusive publishing rights for this book, as well as all others in THE MOTORCYCLIST'S LIBRARY.

Included in THE MOTORCYCLIST'S LIBRARY are complete instruction manuals covering the care and operation of respective motorcycles and engines; valuable data on speed tuning, and thrilling accounts of motorcycle race events. See listing of available titles elsewhere in this edition.

We consider it a privilege to be able to offer so many fine titles to our customers.

FLOYD CLYMER
Publisher of Books Pertaining to Automobiles and Motorcycles

2125 W. PICO ST. LOS ANGELES 6, CALIF.

CONTENTS

CHAP.		PAGE
	PREFACE	
I.	THE PRENTICE HAND	1
II.	DRIVING	13
III.	HOW AN INTERNAL COMBUSTION ENGINE WORKS	32
IV.	LUBRICATION	44
V.	GARAGING AND MAINTENANCE . . .	53
	INDEX	107

CHAPTER I
THE PRENTICE HAND

THE reader is first of all regarded as being a purchaser and nothing else. He has, either by capital outlay or by deposit on an instalment scheme, of which more anon, become possessed of a motor-cycle. If he takes delivery at an agent, which is highly probable, he will be helped in preliminaries by the vendor, who is usually a conscientious and enthusiastic dealer in motor-cycles.

Even so, if this is a book of instruction, it should not release the hand of the pupil and just turn him over to the tender mercies of somebody else. Firstly, the beginner must place himself right with the law by registering the machine. Under the present scheme of taxation, which possesses many anomalies, but which is nevertheless operative, the rider has to pay in advance for the privilege of using the roads. It is first of all necessary that the machine is registered, and before this can be completed it is also necessary that the rider take out a third-party insurance. On the form required (Form R.F. 1/2) he has to quote the make, type, horse-power, numbers of the engine and frame, both of which are marked on the machine, and whether it is used for drawing a sidecar. The duty chargeable has to be paid on application, and, in the case of Rudge machines, with the exception of the 250 c.c., is £3 15s. for a solo machine for a year's licence or £1 0s. 8d. for a quarter's licence. With sidecar fitted the tax is £5 and £1 7s. 7d. respectively. In the case of the 250 c.c. machines tax is £1 17s. 6d. per annum, or 10s. 4d. for the quarter's licence. The slight extra cost of paying quarterly represents a facility for those to whom the outlay of the whole amount is a burden; but in cases where the yearly sum can be paid without inconvenience, I strongly advocate it. There are two specific reasons for this advice. There is the fact that one does not have to undertake the formalities necessary to renewal as each quarter-day comes round. This may not appear to be important, but it is surprising how easy it is to forget to make the renewal or to procrastinate. There is also this: a motor-cyclist who has a yearly licence is "franked" for the four seasons. He does not have to consider whether it is worth while to take out a licence for, say, the January to March period. Motor-cycling is an all-season pastime and there are, during the winter months, hard and crisp days when riding is extremely pleasant, when the tang of tonic air is more enjoyable than the warmth of the summer. To steal a day in the open on a fine winter's day is one of the greatest charms which the saddle has to offer. The man who, paying his taxation quarterly, has omitted to cover himself for the first three months of the year, invariably experiences regret on what is known as a "hunting" morning. It is worth going the whole hog on registration fees, because your machine is always ready for the road; the pistol is always loaded as it were, and you cannot run out of ammunition at a time when you badly want to shoot.

The machine must be re-registered with the local authority, that is, the local borough or county council. The application may be personal or by post, and in return for the payment the

Fig. 1. The 250 c.c. "Rapid" Model (Two-Valve)

local authority will issue a registration licence disc containing letters and numerals, the letters denominating the district, and the figures your number on a local register. The application form must be accompanied by a cover-note or a certificate of insurance, and the registration book. If you are a "learner," you must fit "L" plates. You are now qualified as far as the machine is concerned. The local authorities, and through them, the police, have you marked down, for you are the owner and the responsible person in respect to the motor-cycle, which has been registered in your name. In addition to the licence disc, you will have returned to you the registration book. This is very largely a title-deed on your property. Possession of it denotes, and could legally prove, ownership of the machine. It is therefore imperative that you should retain this. Do not carry it on the machine so that it can be stolen or lost with it. Keep it at home in your garage or in some such place of safety. If and when you come to sell your machine, the registration book is your guarantee of ownership and goodwill. Because it contains the date of registration of your machine, it protects the buyer against fraud, for it discloses the year of your machine's birth.

The Driving Licence. It is now necessary for you to obtain an annual driving licence, which costs 5s. and is obtainable if you are over 16. If you have held a recent annual licence or have held one prior to 1st April, 1934, you must fill up Form DLI and post it, together with the fee of 5s. and the old licence, to the licensing authorities, in exchange for which you will receive the new licence, which you must sign. All applicants for driving licences now have to sign a declaration on the application form as to

Fig. 2. The 250 c.c. "Sports" Model (Two-Valve)

physical fitness (including good eyesight). If you have never before, or not prior to 1st April, 1934, held a licence you will have to pass a driving test and should apply for a three-months' provisional licence (see page 31) to enable you to learn to drive. The cost of the provisional licence is 5s. and of the test 10s. You will be required to provide a machine on which the test is to be made, and on passing the test you must obtain the annual driving licence, which costs another 5s.

It is illegal to be in charge of a motor-cycle unless you have actually taken out a driving licence. Any motor-cyclist is at any time liable to stoppage by a policeman, who is entitled to ask to see his licence without assigning any reason therefor, and if he is unable to produce it, it is necessary that he should do so *in person* within five days at any police station he specifies.

Insurance. As previously stated, it is necessary by law that the rider be insured against third-party risks, but it is recommended that the new rider should take out a comprehensive insurance policy with a tariff company. The cost thereof is not excessive, and it represents a definite expenditure by way of cover against accidents and all that may be occasioned thereby. Far better to know and to pay a definite sum than to take the risk, however small that risk may be, of being seriously impoverished.

Comprehensive insurance with a Rudge would be somewhere in the region of nine to ten pounds. It should be written off as a first charge on motor-cycling. By law the rider is responsible,

FIG. 3. THE 500 C.C. "SPECIAL" MODEL

and the insurance company which accepts his premium is really a financial backer. But insurance means that the ramifications of a big organization are behind you in any claim which may be made upon you. Since this book is dedicated primarily to the new rider, I would urge with all my heart the advisability of comprehensive insurance. In doing so, I am delivering myself of the soundest advice.

Sport or Pastime. The majority of motor-cyclists regard the pursuit as a pastime, and buy their machines for touring purposes. There is quite a considerable sporting side to the movement, however, and many clubs are in existence which organize such events as reliability trials. I do not propose to deal with the sporting side because the beginner will very soon find the social and sporting environment which suits him. I would advise membership of a local club because of the valuable help and comradeship which club-life brings. Even if the social or sporting side does not greatly interest you, the comradeship and willing assistance with which your fellow club members accord you will be very acceptable.

There are also national organizations to be considered. Should a new rider join the Automobile Association, the Royal Automobile Club, or the Auto Cycle Union? The last-named is now only concerned with the sporting side and may be disregarded in the early stages of motor-cycling. The A.A. and the R.A.C. afford facilities which, at the fee charged for membership, are ridiculously cheap. Each has a special motor-cyclist's department, which is under the control of an enthusiast. It exists for the welfare of motor-cyclists, and offers legal defence, considerable

Fig. 4. The 500 c.c. "Sports Special" Model with Upswept Exhaust Pipes

touring facilities, etc. An army of well-trained road scouts is at the service of members.

The Automobile Association is a very fine institution, and well worthy of support, but it is not my intention to advise the newcomer to join everything and anything which is available. For a start, I think he will do well to join the R.A.C. or A.A.

Buying Second-hand. Now as to purchase. Should the beginner—and I will assume that he is a man who is not so well blessed with this world's riches as to be unmindful of expenditure —buy a third-hand or a second-hand mount? I think the latter. There is a certain amount of guarantee as to serviceability when a used machine is purchased from a reputable dealer, but when the deal goes through this channel the price must be very adjacent to market value. Big bargains, colloquially known as "snippets," are not for the beginner, for the purchase must be speculative, and the less the buyer knows about the machine, the less attractive is the speculation. Buying through a well-known firm of dealers with a reputation to lose, is a gilt-edged investment, with all the attractiveness of safety, and none of the attractiveness of the really big bargain. But I am no lover of third-hand buying. It seems to me like buying a mature dog instead of a puppy. It may sound strange to the raw hand, who does not appreciate how " matey " one may become with a motor-cycle, but it is the fact that a certain affinity can exist between

Fig. 5. The 1933–6 Rudge 500 c.c. "Special" Power Unit

 A = Magneto table clamping nuts
 C = Oil tell-tale
 J = Pilot jet adjuster screw
 K = Clutch adjuster lock-nut
 N = Gearbox filler plug
 P = Set pin (pump plunger)
 S = Push-rod cover

the human and dead metal. A rider can get to have a warm regard for his mount, and that regard can never be the same with several men's leavings.

If economy is essential, there is an alternative to cash down buying in the deferred payment or hire-purchase scheme. To pay for a thing by instalments means that instead of paying from capital, one is paying from income. By its general adoption, motor-cycles, in common with houses, furniture, in fact almost every expensive commodity, come within the purchasing scope of a community, which, without it, would be debarred from the enjoyment thereof. There is some prejudice against H.P. payments, but is there any sound reason why a man should not be permitted to pay for an article from his income ? It is absolutely necessary that the purchaser should limit the amount of his payments to such sums as he can comfortably afford, but if this is done, I see nothing against the instalment plan. There are many thousands of people who cannot spend £60 in a cash sum, but who can very well afford to pay the monthly instalments which are charged when that sum is stretched over 12–18

Fig. 6. The 1937-9 Rudge 500 c.c. "Special" Power Unit
Note the improved rocker-box design with exterior oil feed pipe
The gearbox apron is shown removed

A = Oil tell-tale
B = Set screw (pump plunger)
C = Plugs (oil pump)
D = Clutch adjuster lock-nut
E = Magneto table clamp nuts
F = Dynamo strap bolts

months. Second-hand machines are obtainable on an easy scheme of payments, and I would advise participation in this scheme in preference to the purchase of a third-hand mount which might or might not be satisfactory, which may have been roughly treated, and is possibly in poor mechanical condition.

I realize that this advocacy will not break down the barriers of those who are dogmatically opposed to easy payments. To those I would say, most emphatically : Do not buy a second-hand machine from an unknown owner, even with the assistance of a self-styled or actual expert. Pay the little extra which is entailed by dealing with a good firm of dealers. It is safer and better. Time enough when you are a fully fledged and experienced roadfarer to consult small ads. for big bargains. For the time being you are a fledgling. Do not lose sight of the fact, when you are budgeting on instalment payments that you must also set aside, or consider, running costs and general charges, such as garaging, insurance, taxation. Do not bite off more than you can chew. Allow yourself an ample margin, and if the payments admit of this, do not fear that there is any stigma attaching to the easy payment scheme of purchase. It is honest, fair and convenient. Many people who can well afford capital payment prefer to accept the facility of purchase rendered possible by modern methods. It pays them to purchase out of income rather than to disturb invested money.

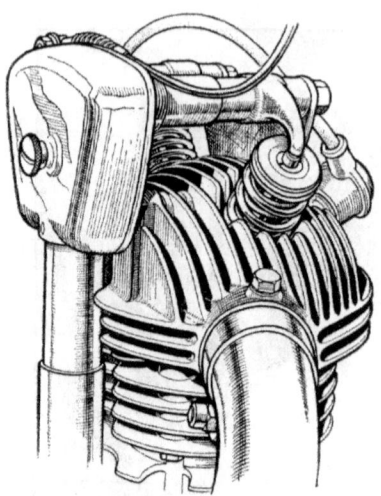

FIG. 7. THE CYLINDER HEAD AND VALVE-GEAR OF THE 250 C.C. TWO-VALVE ENGINE

This engine is fitted on the 1935 "Tourist," the 1936-8 "Rapid," and the 1937-9 250 c.c. "Sports," and is the only one having two instead of four valves; 1937-9 engines have a finned exhaust nut

(*From "The Motor Cycle"*)

Depreciation. A well-kept motor-cycle will not depreciate so quickly as one which is neglected, and if and when the time comes for disposing of the machine second-hand a better price will be obtainable if the exterior appearance provides an idea of the careful manner in which the vendor has kept the whole machine. This matter of second-hand buying is not of considerable importance, however, because the market value of a second-hand machine, though not quite definite, varies only to a small degree. But, in the reliable use of the machine, depreciation does matter a lot. There is no reason why a Rudge, if well cared for, should not last several years without requiring overhaul. Wear is inevitable, and it will be necessary at times to renew bearings, but maintenance charges, which are very largely governed by the rate of depreciation, will be less in proportion to the care bestowed on the machine.

RUNNING COSTS

There have been many attempts to arrive at an approximate figure indicating the cost of running different types of motorcycles, but these may be disregarded. It is safe to budget on a maximum charge of about 2d. a mile, including all extraneous costs, so far as a solo Rudge is concerned. But if you are careless, or unfortunate, the cost will run much higher. This mileage cost should not be regarded as an actual charge, because it is right to offset something against it. Motor-cycling is a pastime

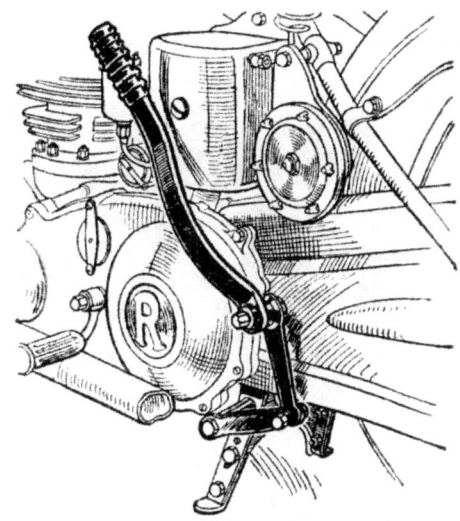

Fig. 8. Useful for Parking—The Hand-operated Central Stand

The stand shown is fitted as standard on all the 500 c.c. models

(*From "The Motor Cycle"*)

and a sport. Most young men spend something on pleasure, and while they are operating at, shall we say, a penny a mile, they are paying about one shilling and eightpence for an hour's pleasure. Had that hour been devoted to some other pleasure there would have been an incurred expense, which would perhaps absorb that sum, which might exceed it, and which certainly would give us a set-off sum. It may be taken as a general rule that mileage costs rise with the average speed. The man who normally averages twenty miles an hour does not pay so much for his consumables, which are petrol, oil, and tyres, as the more hectic type of rider, who likes to open his throttle wide, and enjoy that intoxicating pleasure of travelling at high speed. In seeking economy, the rider should avoid risks. For example, it would be unwise to run tyres to destruction when they are so badly worn as to occasion frequent punctures and render a burst probable; it would be unwise to delay changing the oil which is circulated by the dry sump pump. After a time the oil becomes dirty and contaminated, and frequent changing of this oil will give better performance with less rate of wear on the engine parts. Too great an insistence on economy is to rob motor-cycling of much of its charm, and the man who cannot properly afford to run a motor-cycle is better off without a machine.

Fig. 9. Ideal for Fast Touring—The 500 c.c. "Ulster" Model (Aluminium-Bronze Head)

The now famous "Ulster" was undoubtedly the "star" of the Rudge programme. With its powerful engine having special alloy cylinder head, enclosed pressure lubricated semi-radial valve gear, special cylinder and massive crankcase, it is a mount combining superb performance with reliability and economy

Reliability, which is born in the factory and nursed in the garage, is the patron of economy.

TOURING

Motor-cycling has come to be of great utilitarian value to those who seek economic transport, but primarily it is a means of touring, and the motor-cycle is a unit of pleasure before it is one of industry. Some riders much prefer to tour in haphazard fashion than to arrange a detailed and predestined journey with definite ideas as to when and where stops will be made. It would be idle to declare that either method is preferable to the other. There is a wondrous charm about taking the machine out for a day in the country and travelling willy-nilly, with never a thought or a care as to the road which is to be followed. Trips of exploration along unknown byways are delightful, and fall more easily to the motor-cyclist than the motorist, owing to the tractability and controllability of the machine. Rides with an object have this to commend them: that there is always a prearranged goal, and that, the destination having been settled, the matter of accommodation, etc., is out of mind. When the trip or tour is mapped out and reduced to time-tables and schedules it is unwise to budget on too high an average speed. Touring is not nearly so enjoyable as it might be when a difficult schedule has to be adhered to. Twenty miles an hour or so is a fair average for any other than a forced march, for conformity therewith permits of occasional wayside halts. For holiday touring, it is not a bad plan to have a general idea as to the area of touring and leave actual resting-places to consideration of time, weather, and inclination. To travel and to stop when and where fancy dictates is to enjoy roadfaring at its best, and I do not, for this reason, advocate the hard and fast touring plan and holiday chart.

Touring facilities are to be obtained from membership of the Royal Automobile Club or the Automobile Association, but such is the mobility of the motor-cycle, that the rider need not worry about available accommodation. He can usually find bed and board whenever they are desired.

SECOND-HAND SALE

In course of time the rider may require to sell his machine second-hand. There is an extraordinary fetish among motor-cyclists, as a result of which the second-hand market is a very much more active one than would be supposed. Many motor-cyclists dispose of their machines after one, two, or three years' use, though there is really no reason why a well-kept machine should not be retained by its owner for a much greater period. One thing which has tended toward this constant selling and buying is that the tide of evolution has gone on and on, so that in a space of three years a motor-cycle has become "old-fashioned," if not "obsolete." There is a sign that this state of affairs is likely to change very shortly; indeed, there are prospects that the pace of evolution will not be as high in the future as it has been in the past. When the machine is disposed of the owner has the alternative of selling to a private buyer or of using the machine in connection with the purchase of a new motor-cycle or car. In the latter case the full market value of the machine is usually obtainable, and if the owner intends to acquire another vehicle he may confidently operate the part-exchange scheme which obtains. In selling a motor-cycle privately the vendor should be careful not to permit the potential buyer to " try her out " unless he has some guarantee of good faith. It is easy to ride away on a machine which has been handed over for trial, but not so easy to trace a machine once it has got into the hands of those wily bilkers who play on the credulity of honest people.

Never forget that your registration book is, in effect, a title-deed to the machine, and that it should not be handed over to a purchaser until the deal has finally been completed. When you are satisfied that you have received payment for the machine—not merely a cheque—you may hand over the registration book, but not before. You must also notify the change of ownership to the licensing authority in writing. The new owner must also do this and return the registration book to the licensing authority in whose area he will normally keep the machine.

CHAPTER II
DRIVING

Getting Ready. After seeing that both the number plates (see page 26) and registration licence are in accordance with legal requirements, the reader will, naturally, be anxious to test the capabilities of the machine on the road. He would be wise, however, to inspect the machine carefully on several points. First of all, make quite sure that the oil tank contains suitable oil, preferably of the brand recommended by the makers. In the case of the standard machines, apart from racing models, the following are recommended: Castrol Grand Prix, Shell X–100 SAE 50 (SAE 40 during winter), Mobiloil D (BB during winter), Price's Energol SAE 50, and Essolube 50 (40 during winter). For 1936–9 "Ulster" models Essolube Racer is the correct grade. The gearbox, too, is often delivered without oil, in which case the filler cap on the right-hand side of the machine, just below the kick-starter, should be removed, and any of the above grades of oil should be used to fill up to the level of the filler cap. Replenish with a premium grade petrol or 50/50 benzol mixture ("Ulster" engines).

The reader should then familiarize himself with the controls, and Fig. 12 shows the controls fitted to Rudge machines. It will be seen that, on the right side of the handlebars, there is the front brake, the air lever, and a twist-grip throttle control. The throttle is opened by turning the twist-grip inwards. The air lever also opens inwards and should be left in this position when the engine is running. On all 1935–9 Rudge models a "dimmer" switch is also fitted on this side. On the left side of the bars there is a dummy twist-grip to match the throttle twist-grip, and a pair of levers of the brake lever type. The exhaust lifter is the outer one, and is only for starting and stopping the engine. This leaves the clutch lever in a convenient position for use when changing gear. In front of this is the ignition lever, which retards and advances the spark, an inward movement of the lever being required for the advance position. There is also the headlamp switch, mounted on the lamp, which is marked "Off," "C," "H," and "L"; "Off" representing the "Off" position when no current is being supplied; "C" for charge being used when no lights are required and the battery needs charging; "H" for full head, side, tail lights; and "L" for the dim bulb in the head light, required for parking purposes. There remains then the gear control gate on the tank. With the lever in the forward position, first, or bottom, gear is engaged. The neutral position is between first and second gear, fourth gear being engaged when the lever is nearest to the saddle. On the 500 c.c. models a decompressor lever is fitted on the timing cover and moved outwards to operate.

When a foot gear control is fitted this is so arranged that, when the pedal is operated downward to its limit, a higher gear is engaged, and an upward movement changes to a lower gear. A

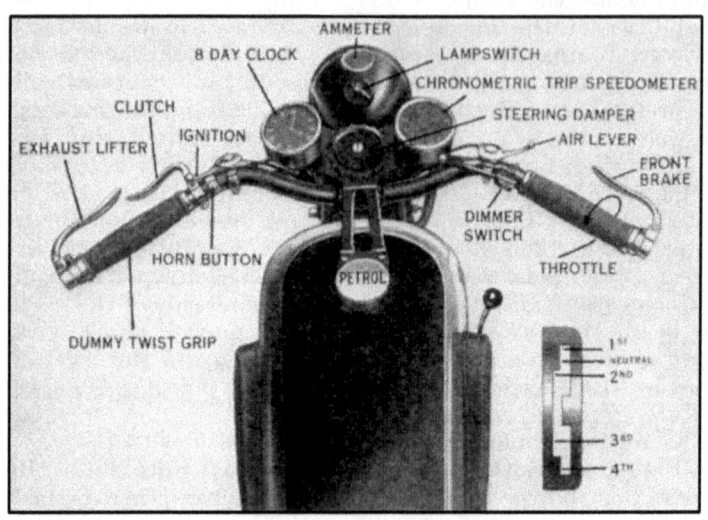

FIG. 10. THE 1935 RUDGE CONTROLS
A decompressor is fitted on the timing cover on 500 c.c. engines
The 1933–4 control layout is similar to that shown (see Fig. 12)

circular disc with the gear positions marked is fitted to the step-by-step mechanism on the side of the gearbox on some 250 c.c. models, and a pointer indicates which gear is engaged, so that inspection will show when the gear is in neutral.

Before actually running the machine on the road the reader will find it very useful to start up the machine when on the stand, and accustom himself to the feel of the controls and gear changing, so that there shall be no doubt in his mind, when the machine is actually on the road, in which direction to operate the controls. The position of the brake should also be carefully noted, so that, in an emergency, no delay will occur in bringing the machine to rest. To start up from cold, flood carburettor, close air lever and open throttle $\frac{1}{8}$–$\frac{1}{4}$. Retard ignition $\frac{1}{2}$, operate decompressor (where fitted) and kick the engine over. If only an exhaust-valve lifter is provided, raise this and drop it when the kickstarter is

DRIVING

half way down. Release the decompressor as soon as the engine fires and do not run the engine with the machine stationary for more than a few minutes.

In starting away bottom gear should be engaged. After the machine has gathered speed a change up to second gear should be made. To do this, speed up the machine, throttle down, lift the clutch lever and make a smart movement of the gear control lever into the second gear. A noiseless change can thus be made. A similar procedure is adopted for third and top gears, the top gear being required when the machine has attained a speed of about 25 m.p.h. Changing down is done in a similar manner, but in this case the throttle should be closed and the engine speeded up with the clutch out just before changing.

The four-speed gearbox will be found a very useful item in the specification, since the third gear is high enough to attain a very useful range of speed, even under somewhat hilly conditions, and, for this reason, a good driver will adopt the procedure of using gears when circumstances require it. There is really no need to use the ignition lever in order to slog up a hill in top gear when the third speed would really be much more suitable for the engine and would permit a higher speed with less strain on the engine.

The brakes on Rudge machines are of a very effective type, and on some the foot lever operates both front and rear brakes. By means of a clever device incorporated in the rear brake mechanism, the proper amount of braking is given to both front and rear wheels under all degrees of braking, so that the rider need have little fear of skidding if the amount of braking is applied with even less than the normal respect for slippery surfaces. In addition to this, the hand brake lever can apply a further braking effect to the front wheel when really hard braking is found necessary, such as when descending severe hills or in cases of emergency.

With a renovated machine the best results can only be obtained by exercising care in the early period of driving. No attempt should be made to drive the machine at more than one-third throttle for 500 miles and one-half throttle for 1,000 miles in order to give the working parts an opportunity of bedding down. In spite of extreme care in the manufacture of all the rubbing parts, it is quite impossible to obtain the glass-like finish which will result if the machine is run carefully over the initial period.

ROAD SENSE

Common-sense Riding. Although recent legislation has involved us in many rules and regulations (and a summary of these is given later), these will not worry anyone who uses common sense and thinks of the other fellow. Road sense is a combination of common sense and experience, with due regard for others on the road.

The modern motor-cycle is possessed of such facility of control that it immediately and directly is responsive to the rider's requirements. All things mechanical are, and must be, subservient to the human brain, and it is the rider and not the machine which is the more prone to mistakes.

The fact that a machine is capable of travelling at sixty, seventy or eighty miles an hour means that it may be, as a result of recklessness, a power of great evil ; but so long as the human machine functions properly, it is not in the very least degree dangerous. That is why common sense is the most important factor in motor-cycling. It is not common sense to drive at such a speed that the machine cannot be stopped within the range of uninterrupted visibility. To put it plainer. When a motor-cyclist is driving there is always a certain amount of empty road ahead of him. The limit of safe speed is that which permits him to bring his machine to a standstill within that empty space. All things which suggest the possibility of interrupting the empty space, such as the entrance to a house, a side turning, an approaching vehicle, or even a dog, must be regarded as hazards.

Common sense could not under any circumstances permit a rider to pass a cross-road at any speed other than a crawl ; nor could it allow a man to alter the direction of his travel without warning any possible followers of his intention of so doing. There is no law which requires a rider to signal, but it would be foolish not to do so, and in the event of an accident, the erring rider might be liable under the general clause of driving to the common danger.

There are certain defined and generally accepted signals which all roadfarers should, but do not, observe. Two of them are set out in Fig. 11. If you intend stopping, swing your right arm slowly backwards and forwards to indicate to the man behind that he may proceed beyond you ; but do not do this unless the road ahead is clear, otherwise you are leading another man into trouble. If the road ahead is obstructed, as by one vehicle overtaking another while approaching you, stretch your right arm out horizontally to apprise following traffic of the danger ahead. Such acts of courtesy tend towards the general safety, and though not compulsory, are advisable. Undoubtedly the greatest menace of all is the uncontrolled cross-road. In my experience of roadfaring under all conditions, I have seen more bad driving and more accidents at cross-roads than at any other hazard. The right of way morally belongs to the man who is on the more important of the roads which cross, but that does not permit the man on the highway to " blind " over the crossing

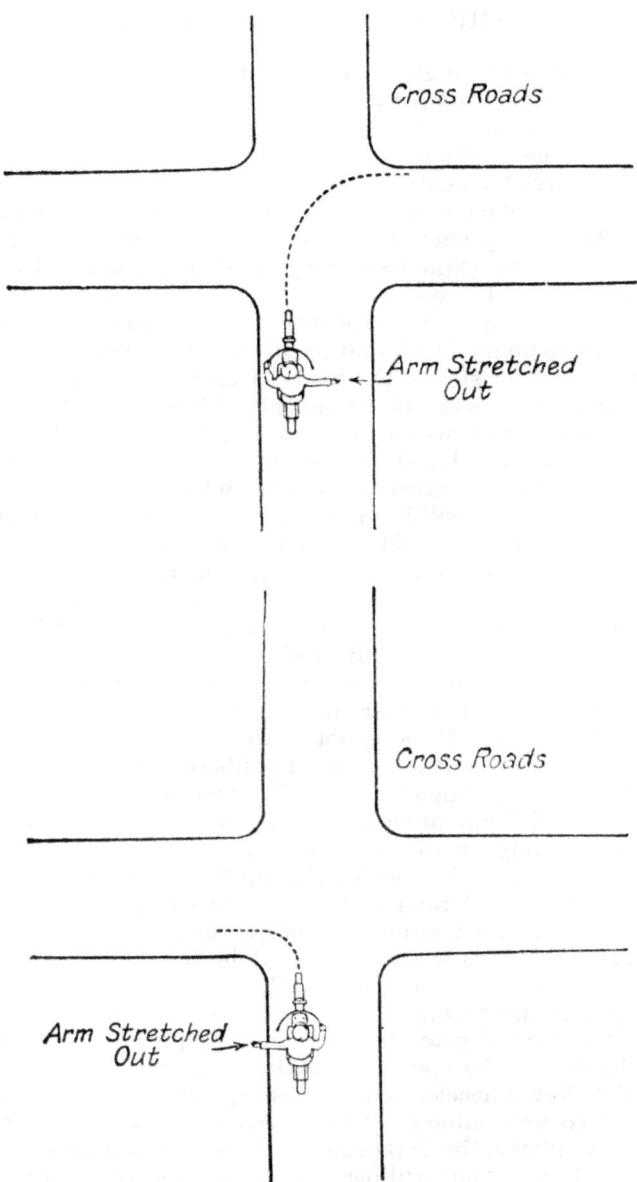

FIG. 11. TRAFFIC SIGNALS TO USE AT CORNERS

The official signal for "I am going to turn left" is now to extend the right arm horizontally and rotate it from the shoulder anti-clockwise. The signal shown is, however, quite suitable for motor-cyclists regardless of what might be on the other road. The maximum speed at which a cross-road should be passed is ten miles an hour. Nine times out of ten you may cross with impunity at twenty, the tenth time might make you pay a heavy price for the nine times you have " chanced your arm." Another source of danger is the humpbacked bridge which cuts out visibility beyond its brow. Never approach such a bridge at speed. A bad driver on the other side might be passing another vehicle, and in doing so close the road to you.

Never, under any circumstances, try to pass another man while approaching a bend, and on all curves, however slight, keep well into the near side of the road. Observe the white line rule, and do not trespass on the wrong side of the line or "catseyes."

There is no reason why you should not, in areas not "built up," indulge in speed. There are absolutely safe stretches of road which entice you to travel fast and upon which the enticement is no snare. It is not within my province to advocate or to encourage speeding, but I would say that the road hog or the selfish rider is not he who indulges in an occasional speed sprint, but he who is unmindful of the welfare and the nerves of the general community by riding faster than he should through "built up" areas where there is the slightest element of danger.

Follow the nautical axiom, slow speed in a fog, regarding everything but an absolutely clear and open road as fog.

Seeking Silence. Noise is not so much a matter of deficiency in the design of motor-cycles as of deliberate ostentation on the part of riders. If a machine is well driven it need not be objectionable at all; but obviously it can become a nuisance if the rider deliberately creates a disturbance. Do not unnecessarily " race " your engine by opening the throttle control too wide when starting. The good rider is he who can roll away quietly and gently, the bad rider is he who makes his engine roar, slams in his gear, and " tells the world " that he is about to start on a tour. It is in the nature of youth to be noisy, but I would strongly urge my young readers to avoid the demonstrative. A dignified and quiet getaway is far more impressive than a noisy one. Excess in the operation of the controls should always be avoided. Never accelerate or increase your speed too suddenly. In doing so you subject all the mechanical parts to abnormal strain. Similarly, the brakes should be regarded as an emergency control. There is more rubber worn from tyres by excessive braking than is necessary. Never, except under necessity, should the road-wheels be locked. To ride up to your destination at speed and come to rest with a staccato jerk as a result of hard braking is damaging both to the machine and to your own reputation.

SOME DRIVING HINTS

The beginner will find that his machine is a very tractable and obedient piece of machinery, and he will very quickly master the various controls. But the employment of those controls in different circumstances is another matter. Along a straight and level road, he may practise until he regards himself as quite capable of undertaking a tour, but the roads are not always straight and level.

The need for using the controls is greater, as the roads become winding or hilly. Let us go with our novice to the first corner, which we will assume is a right-handed one. On approaching it he will slow down by closing the throttle grip. As his machine travels slower he will put out his right arm to signify his intention of turning, and on assuring himself that the coast is clear, he will describe a wide arc which will take him into the turning on the right-hand side. In the event of there being an overtaking vehicle, whose driver is not, apparently, going to heed the signal, he will stop his machine and permit the selfish one to pass. Now, how will he stop his machine? Having closed his throttle to slow down for the turn, his engine will not be turning over very quickly. He will gently apply his brakes and lift his clutch control lever. He will then drop into first or bottom gear, and, when the coast is clear, gradually release his clutch lever and proceed.

Now, let us take our novice to a steep hill and instruct him as to procedure on the brow. Before him the road descends steeply into the valley. His brakes are good enough to hold him on the gradient, but he should not rely on them entirely.

The engine makes an excellent brake when road speed is greater than that of propelled speed. For example: When driving along the level, the engine propels the road wheels at speeds in accordance with the throttle opening. If the throttle is closed right off the engine will stop. On a decline, the road wheels want to revolve of their own accord, owing to gravity. They can be held in check by the engine, for if the throttle is closed the engine will have to be driven by the road wheels through the transmission. Thus, the engine becomes a drag on the wheels. The gear to be employed must be determined by the gradient itself. On a very steep, downward hill, bottom gear should be in operation. The machine cannot then run away, and there is less strain and wear on the brakes which can, by gentle pressure, be made to hold the machine.

If, while climbing a hill, the engine is stopped—only a novice would do this—the restart should carefully be undertaken. Still remaining astride, lift the clutch lever sufficiently to permit the machine gradually to move backwards until the rear wheel is held by a kerb or bank.

Automatic Traffic Lights. These are now extensively used at road junctions and should be obeyed unhesitatingly. Never attempt to cross when you know the "stop" signal is imminent as this may cause a serious crash.

In Fig. 13 is shown an automatic traffic light signal of the three-light pattern, and these are in use in all big towns.

Red by itself means "Stop" on reaching line.

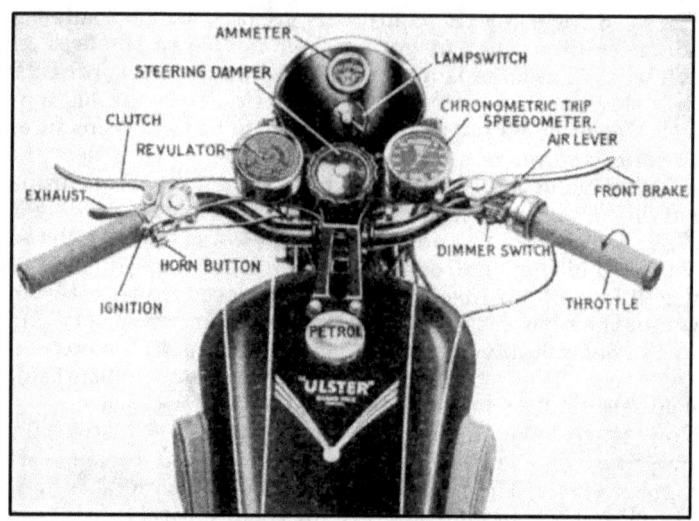

FIG. 12. THE 1936 RUDGE CONTROLS

As previously, a decompressor is fitted on the timing case of 500 c.c. engines. Inverted type exhaust lifter and front brake levers have been dropped and the 8-day clock has been omitted in favour of a "Revulator" on "Special" and "Ulster" models. The controls on all 1937–9 Rudges are similar to those shown, but a "Revulator" is not provided

Amber together with *red*, means "Prepare to start."

Green is the all-clear signal, indicating that the driver can proceed in safety. *Amber* alone means "Stop on the line unless you had crossed it when *amber* appeared."

Skidding. The Rudge machine is famous for its tractability and easy steering qualities. Skids are not thus to be feared by riders, but it is as well to be prepared for them. Skidding is occasioned by the loss of frictional resistance between the road wheels and the road surface, as by frozen roads, mud or grease. It is a rider's first instinct to put on his brakes when he discovers his machine to be getting out of control. This is just what should not be done in a skid, for it amplifies the lateral tendency of the skidding wheel by turning it into a skate. If the rear wheel slides away, the front wheel should be turned in the same direction. Skidding is very largely caused by sudden alterations of speed on wet and greasy roads, and when the underwheel conditions are conducive to skidding an even pace should be maintained all the time. In traffic as wide a berth as possible should be given to every other road user, and, with the Rudge machine, third speed should be engaged. This offers an ideal ratio for traffic work.

Pillion Riding. A great deal has been written and said of pillion riding recently, and the practice has been greatly maligned. At a time when motor-cycles were less tractable than they are to-day there was a pronounced element of danger in the conveyance of a passenger on a rear carrier which was not sufficiently strong for the weight imposed, but the sturdy and well-balanced later design of machines makes pillion riding a much safer proposition, particularly with a properly designed and fitted pillion seat, such as the law now requires. Obviously it is unwise to take as passenger on the pillion anybody who is of such nervous temperament as to be likely to interfere with the control of the machine. But if the passenger regards himself or herself as no more than a passenger, and if the rider is careful, there is no more danger than when the machine is being ridden solo. In point of fact, the additional weight on the back can, in certain circumstances, enhance safety. On a treacherously greasy road I would prefer to ride with rather than without a pillion passenger. It should be noted that pillion passengers must ride astride on a seat *fixed* to the machine (*see also* page 30).

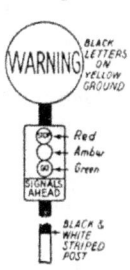
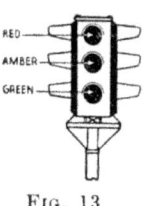

Fig. 13

Night Riding. This can be very fascinating, particularly when the roads are clear, but, under modern conditions, demands considerable care on the part of the rider. The cyclist is decidedly difficult to see when the motor-cyclist is confronted by the glare of two powerful head-lights fitted to an oncoming car. The regulations regarding the fitting of a rear lamp are not always observed by cyclists, and one cannot depend, therefore, upon seeing the light which an efficient and properly fitted lamp would produce.

A dazzling head-light is very dangerous and calls for very careful driving. Never take risks. Do not assume that there is nothing on the road ahead; be certain that there is not, or else stop altogether. It is no defence to say that you were blinded by head-lights, for it is your first duty to know that the road ahead is free of other traffic, and the onus of responsibility, by road law, always rests with the overtaking vehicle or machine.

Night riding in rural districts is rendered more dangerous by the fact that one must always be prepared to encounter straying cattle. Speed should be limited to clarity of vision, and safe speed is dependent on the power of your headlamp. Although the law does not require you to light up until half an hour after sunset, it is wise to light up well before then. The gloaming is the most dangerous period of the day. Roadfarers who, like the Foolish Virgins, have not troubled to have their lamps in order, may be hurrying home in order to dispense with the necessity of lighting up. In doing so they take a risk, and that risk is shared by you unless your own machine is conspicuous in the treacherous light of the dusk. Switch on your lamps as soon as you feel that the occasion warrants it. Where a lead-acid accumulator is employed, this should always be kept in good condition. It should be topped-up monthly (*see* page 85) and regularly charged by day (*see* page 86), so that there is never a chance of your being caught in the darkness without being able to light up.

Electric Lighting. Electric lighting is provided on the majority of pre-war Rudge motor-cycles and comprises Miller dynamo lighting equipment, or in some instances a Lucas Maglita set. Both lighting sets are very reliable and require practically no attention, apart from the necessity of seeing that the accumulator is "flush." Distilled water should be poured carefully into the accumulator until plates are just covered, to make up for evaporation.

A Useful Book. A book in this series strongly recommended to all Rudge owners is *The Art of Motor-cycling*. This deals in much detail with preparing for the road, preliminaries, accessories, clothing, learning to ride, the technique of riding, the driving tests, touring at home and abroad, etc.

A FEW DON'TS

Never give the " other fellow " too much credit for roadmanship. Always be ready for his mistakes.

Don't forget your oil. Lubrication is the life's blood of an internal combustion engine. Watch the "tell-tale."

Also, remember the motor-cycle bearings. They too must be kept well lubricated.

Don't swank. Pride comes before a fall in motor-cycling more than in anything else.

Don't assume that the road round the corner is clear. Always take the line that it is blocked to you.

Don't forget that your gearbox is there for a purpose and not as an ornament.

Don't use your brakes too often. Regard them as emergency controls only.

DRIVING

Remember that the throttle is the best of all controls for varying road speeds. The exhaust lifter should not be used, except for starting the engine.

Don't try her out unless the road is an absolutely safe and clear one and don't ride "hands off" (police strongly object).

Don't argue about road rights with a policeman. He knows the law better than you do, and he can enforce it.

Regard the white line as a boundary over which you must not trespass.

Don't procrastinate on refuelling. Always have plenty of oil and petrol.

Don't neglect your machine. An hour in the garage means many trouble-free miles on the road.

Don't let your tyres get slack. Keep them correctly inflated.

Don't just think the pressure is right. Test it with a good gauge.

Don't indulge in excessive speed, which is entirely different from fast speed.

Don't ignore road signs. You may be painfully reminded of what they are there for.

PRECAUTIONARY MEASURES

Experienced road riders invariably and instinctively look over their machines before taking them on the road. With their expert eyes they cursorily can examine their machines and satisfy themselves that they are as roadworthy as possible.

Licence. See that your registration licence is properly fixed. Carry driving licence, insurance "Certificate," or cover note.

Petrol. See that you have plenty of petrol in the tank. It is irksome to interrupt a run, and more than irksome to run out of " juice " with no petrol pump nearby.

Engine Oil. See that the oil tank beside the seat pillar is well filled. The mechanical oiling will do the rest (*see* page 45).

Tyres. If you have time, run your eyes over the treads and remove any flinty stones and nails which may not puncture in the first revolution of the wheel. Sometimes a puncture is caused by a nail picked up on the preceding day. You will save many punctures by removing what your tyres have picked up.

Tightness. Wheel the machine for a few yards and give it a shake or two. This might disclose any looseness which can be rectified. See that no controls are slack.

Run your spanner over the nuts and bolts to ascertain tightness.

Transmission. Test for transmission condition. If a chain is loose, retension it. See that it does not run dry and is properly lubricated (*see* page 50).

Lighting Set. Turn the lighting switch to the "H" and "L" positions and note whether the driving, parking, tail, and stop light (where fitted) operate satisfactorily. See that the battery is topped-up correctly (*see* page 85).

Sparking Plug. Make sure that it is clean and has the correct gap (*see* page 78).

General Lubrication. Satisfy yourself that all the cycle parts are correctly oiled or greased (*see* pages 49–52).

Brakes. Examine and test brakes. The adjustment is easy.

PERIODICAL ATTENTIONS (1933-6 MODELS)

Below is given a summary of attentions necessary to keep the machine in good running condition.

Weekly—
CHECK	Oil level in tank
	Oil level in gearbox
	Tyre pressures

Frequently—
CHECK	Tappet adjustment
	Battery acid level
	Brake adjustment
	Clutch adjustment
	Chain adjustment (primary, rear, dynamo, magneto)
GREASE	Forks
	Overhead rockers
	Steering head
OIL	Push-rods
	Brake and gear controls
	Magneto, as instructed on page 48
	Control cables
	Clutch-operating thrust screw

Occasionally—
CHECK	Nuts and bolts
	Contact-breaker gap
	Plug point gap
	Level in oil bath chain case
	Steering head and shackle adjustment
	Ignition and lighting wiring
CLEAN	Petrol filter in tank
	Oil filter in oil tank and in engine
GREASE	Wheels
	Speedometer gearbox
OIL	Saddle pivot

Drain oil tank. Clean filter and replenish with fresh oil about every 2,000 miles. See also chart on page 53.

ROAD LAW AND LORE

Although the rider may now feel that he is well equipped with sufficient knowledge to drive his machine properly under all circumstances, he should be acquainted with the law of the road. The requirements of the Road Traffic Act and subsequent regulations are very numerous, and a summary of the more important of these is given in the following pages. The reader will find that regulations regarding the construction of the machine itself have been properly covered by the makers, but there are a number of other points which must be complied with by the rider himself, and he would be wise to read and observe them carefully. Two of the least known of the new regulations are that relating to the necessity of reporting accidents and that a fine may be imposed if a driving licence is not signed by the owner.

With care the rider will avoid all trouble with the police and accidents, but there is no guarantee that he will be so fortunate as to be able to "pursue the even tenor of his way" without extraneous interruption. The law is, of course, interpreted and administered by the police system. A policeman has certain rights, and though insistence upon these may at times be irksome to the rider, yet he should maintain a tolerant acceptance thereof.

If a policeman asks to examine your licence, permit him to do so. Do not argue the point with him, and try to efface that indignation which so readily mounts. If you are asked to stop by a policeman you must do so. To refrain from doing so is one of the major crimes of the road, and it is heavily punishable. There are occasions, very few and far between, when a policeman makes a mistake or presents a charge which is absolutely unfounded. It is then politic to protect yourself by drastic measures. To give an example: A rider was once stopped by a policeman because he did not obey a certain signal given by the gentleman in blue. Actually he had misinterpreted a very ambiguous signal. But the policeman was short-tempered, and called upon the rider to pull into the side of the road. The rider, in order to avoid any interruption of traffic streams, rode about 80 yd. down the road, propped his machine against the kerb, and came back. The policeman was very vinegary and objectionable, and took profuse notes. The motor-cyclist, within his rights, asked to know what charge would be preferred against him, and was told that he would be reported for driving to the common danger and refusing to stop when called upon. Unwilling to accept such serious charges, the rider insisted on accompanying the policeman to the station and stating his case, and it was as well that he did, for the inspector was given the full and complete facts, and the policeman was admonished for ridiculous behaviour. But had that rider accepted the charges, it might have gone very badly for him in court. That was, of course, an exceptional case, and indicates a policy in extremity, but normally the policeman is very fair-minded, and no useful purpose is served by opposing him.

Accidents. When a motor-cyclist is involved in an accident, however trivial, he is, by law, bound to stop and see that the results of it are communicated to the police, or are of such minor consequences as to occasion no sequel. To cause injury to anybody, and to drive on without informing the police is a crime against the laws of the country and also against decency. Nobody can help an accident, but to try to sneak away from the consequences is loathsome. Always and inevitably the motor-cyclist

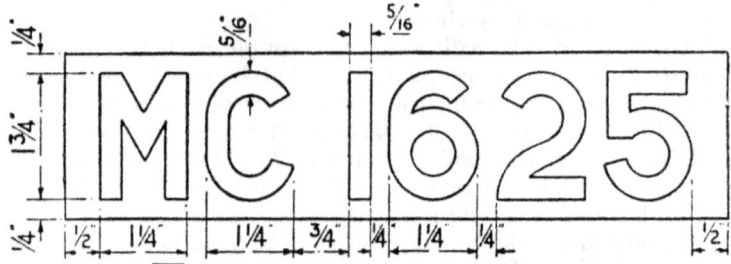

Fig. 14. Front Number Plate Dimensions

should stop after an accident, or when called upon by the police to do so. The observance of road laws can only properly be carried out if these laws are known, and every motor-cyclist should acquaint himself with the provisions of the Road Traffic Act and later amendments made to it.

He who behaves decently and in accordance with the prevailing conditions is not likely seriously to transgress the written statute, and, in any case, he will be a good roadfarer.

Basic Law Points. The most important points to be considered by motor-cyclists are—

Before being entitled to ride, you must have a driving licence, and before the machine is rideable it must have been registered, a third-party insurance taken out, and the inland revenue duty paid.

The registration numbers must be carried on plates in front and behind the machine, and must be distinctly visible from the front or the back of the machine. The number plate characters must be of certain dimensions; those for the front plate (Fig. 14) must be as follows—

Letters and numerals $1\frac{3}{4}$ in. in height and $\frac{5}{16}$ in. thick.

DRIVING

There must be ¼ in. space between the numerals.

The dimensions for the rear number plate (Fig. 15) should be as follows—

(a) All letters and figures must be 2½ in. high; every part of every letter and figure must be ⅜ in. broad; and the total width of the space taken by every letter or figure, except in the case of figure "1," must be 1¾ in.

(b) The space between adjoining letters and between adjoining figures must be ½ in., and there must be a margin of at least ½ in.

Fig. 15. Rear Number Plate Dimensions

between the nearest part of any letter or figure and the top, bottom, and sides of the black background.

Legal highway signs which must be observed are—

Alternate black and white stripes across the road indicate a "Zebra" crossing where pedestrians have right of way.

A "HALT AT MAJOR ROAD AHEAD" sign indicates that you must actually stop, not merely slow down, at the intersection

A "SLOW, MAJOR ROAD AHEAD" sign does not compel you to stop.

The law demands the fitment of two independently working brakes, each of which must be capable of stopping the machine.

You must give audible warning of your approach (see page 29).

No motor-cycle may be left unattended, or in such manner as to cause obstruction. The engine must not be left running when the machine is unattended.

EXTRACTS FROM ROAD TRAFFIC ACT, 1930

Accidents (What to do). Stop immediately. Give name and address and registration number of vehicle, if requested. Failing this, the accident must be reported within 24 hours at a police station or to a police constable.

The Minister of Transport may direct an inquiry to be made into the cause of any accident involving a motor vehicle. A person authorized by the Minister may inspect the vehicle, and at a reasonable time enter premises where vehicle is situated. Obstruction of that person is an offence. The report of an inquiry shall not be used in legal proceedings instituted in consequence of the accident.

Address. If a motorist is alleged to have driven recklessly, dangerously, or carelessly, he must give his name and address to any person having reasonable ground for requiring the information. If he refuses or gives a false name and address, he is guilty of an offence.

Brakes. The machine must be fitted with two independent and efficient brakes.

Careless Driving. A person shall not drive without due care and attention or without reasonable consideration for other road users. A first or second conviction for this offence does not entail disqualification for holding or obtaining a licence.

Dangerous Driving. A person shall not drive recklessly, or at a speed or in a manner dangerous to the public.

Penalties—

Not exceeding £50, or up to four months' imprisonment for the first offence.

Not exceeding £100, or up to four months' imprisonment, or to both such fine and imprisonment for the second or subsequent offence.

Six months' imprisonment or a fine (amount unlimited), or to both such imprisonment and fine, on conviction on indictment. All convictions to be endorsed on the driving licence, with power to disqualify for holding or obtaining a licence.

Driver's Licence. Seventeen is the minimum age for a licence to drive a motor-car, and sixteen for a motor-cycle. No person shall allow another to drive who is not properly licensed. The licence must bear the owner's signature.

A declaration of physical fitness must be made at the time of application. The applicant must also declare that he is not disqualified by age or otherwise from obtaining a licence.

On the request of a police officer, the driver shall produce his licence for examination, to enable the officer to ascertain the name and address of the holder of the licence, the date of issue, and the Authority by which it was issued. If unable immediately to produce the licence, he cannot be convicted of an offence if, within five days of the request for production, he produces the licence *in person* at a police station agreed to by the police.

Drunkenness. Any person convicted of driving, or attempting to drive, or in charge of a motor vehicle on a road or other public place, when under the influence of drink or drugs to such an extent as to be incapable of having proper control of the vehicle, shall be liable—

(a) On summary conviction, to a fine not exceeding £50 or imprisonment up to four months. For a second or subsequent conviction, to a fine not exceeding £100 or up to four months' imprisonment, or to both such fine and imprisonment.

(b) On conviction on indictment, to imprisonment up to six months, or to a fine (unlimited) or to both imprisonment and fine.

A police constable may arrest, without warrant, any person committing this offence.

Unless, for special reasons, the Court thinks otherwise, disqualification for a period of twelve months shall follow a conviction. Particulars of conviction and disqualification shall be endorsed on the driving licence.

Eyesight Test. Are you able to read at a distance of 25 yds. in good daylight (with glasses, if worn) a motor-car number plate containing six letters and figures? Applicants who answer "No" to this question are debarred from obtaining a licence.

Highway Code. The Minister of Transport has prepared a code comprising directions for the guidance of all road users. This code received the approval of both Houses of Parliament, and was printed and issued to the public at one penny per copy.

Failure to observe any provision of the code is not by itself a ground for criminal proceedings of any kind. Nevertheless, it may be relied upon as tending to establish or negative liability in connection with any proceedings, whether civil or criminal.

Horn. A motor vehicle must be fitted with a suitable instrument for giving audible warning of approach where necessary. When a vehicle is stationary on the highway, no person shall use or permit the horn to be used except when such use is necessary on the grounds of safety. See also page 31.

Penalties—

First offence, fine up to £20. Subsequent offences, fine not exceeding £50 or imprisonment up to three months.

Insurance. A person may not use or permit any other person to use a motor vehicle on the road unless such use is covered by insurance against third party claims. This does not require the owner to cover a person in his employ against death or bodily injury arising out of and in the course of his employment—a liability which is covered by other statutes.

Where compensation is paid under the provision of compulsory insurance, and where to the knowledge of the insurer a third party has received hospital treatment, the insurer shall also pay to the hospital a sum not exceeding £25 for each person so treated. This obligation does not apply where a charge has already been made by the hospital.

In addition to the usual policy, or cover note, the insurance company shall hand to the owner a "certificate of insurance" in the prescribed form, and when applying for his motor-cycle licence, the applicant must—by production of the insurance certificate or otherwise—satisfy the Licensing Authority that the necessary cover against third party risks will be in force at the time the motor-cycle licence becomes operative.

The driver of a motor vehicle shall, when requested by a police constable, give his name and address, and produce the insurance certificate. If he cannot produce it immediately, he must produce it *in person* within five days at a police station agreed to by the police officer.

Where an accident occurs involving personal injury to another person, if the driver is unable to produce his certificate at the time, he shall report the accident to a police station as soon as possible, *and in any case within 24 hours of the accident*, and shall there produce his certificate. If the certificate is not available for immediate production, the driver may produce it *in person* within five days at a police station agreed to by the police.

Lights. Motor-cycles with side-cars attached must show two white lights forward (indicating total width), and a red light showing to the rear.

Solo machines must carry one white light in front and a red light at the rear, together with proper illumination of the rear number plate (Fig. 15).

Physical Fitness. A declaration as to physical disabilities must be made by every applicant for a driving licence. This declaration must be in the form prescribed by the Authorities, and it must state whether or not the applicant is suffering from any particular disease or physical disability specified in the form, or from any other disease or disability which would be likely to render it dangerous to drive. If the declaration shows the applicant to be suffering from any such disease or disability, the Licensing Authority can refuse to grant the licence.

Pillion Riding. No more than one person, in addition to the driver, may be carried on a solo motor-cycle, and such person must

DRIVING

sit astride the cycle on a proper seat securely fitted behind the driver's seat and hold a driving licence if the rider is a "learner."

Silence. The motor-cycle must be provided with an expansion chamber, suitable and sufficient for reducing, as far as may be reasonable, the noise which would otherwise be caused by the escape of gas. Also, no person shall use on a road any motor vehicle in such a manner as to cause any excessive noise which could have been avoided by the exercise of reasonable care on the part of the driver.

RECENT LEGISLATION

Driving Tests. As has been mentioned on page 3, new applicants for driving licences and those who have never held a licence prior to 1st April, 1934, or have been exempted from having to take a driving test, must pass a driving test (including knowledge of the Highway Code, an eyesight test, and ability to start, stop, turn and overtake correctly and to give proper hand signals). On conviction for careless or dangerous driving a magistrate may order a driving test. When learning to drive with a provisional licence, which costs 5s., and is valid for 3 months, "L" plates must be fixed to the front and rear of the machine. The form for a driving test is DL26 and this should be filled in and sent with the fee of 10s. to the Supervising Examiner (address on back of form), who will arrange for a test in the nearest convenient area. If you fail first time you can come up again for a test in a month's time. The machine must be provided for the test.

"All Quiet" After 11.30 p.m. The sounding of horns is forbidden between the hours of 11.30 p.m. and 7 a.m., except where necessary to prevent an accident.

30 m.p.h. Speed Limit. A general speed limit of 30 m.p.h. applies to all "built-up" areas, except where otherwise indicated. A "built-up" area is one having a system of street lighting (with the lamps not more than 200 yards apart) or classified as such by the Minister of Transport. In all doubtful cases a circular sign bearing the figure 30 in red on a white background indicates where a 30 m.p.h. limit is in force and another sign indicates where the speed limit ends. Only stop for police *in uniform*.

Pedestrian Crossings. Pedestrians have *absolute* right of way over uncontrolled "Zebra" crossings but they must not loiter. Failure to give an uninterrupted crossing to a pedestrian is a punishable offence and you must not stop on the crossing. Between crossings the same care is necessary as hitherto, for pedestrians are not by law compelled to use the crossings.

CHAPTER III
HOW AN INTERNAL COMBUSTION ENGINE WORKS

I WILL try to explain the working of an internal combustion engine in the simplest possible language. The two components to an explosion, which is the basic cause of power, are an explosive gas and a spark which ignites it. The engine is called an internal combustion engine because the heat energy is created inside the engine itself. Roughly this is what happens: The petrol in your tank is fed through a carburettor which is fitted with a jet from which a little spout of liquid petrol is sprayed. This mixes with air, and is turned into an explosive gas. This is then carried into the combustion chamber where it is fired by a spark. The explosion forces down a piston which is connected to a crank, and this crank converts the up and down movement of the piston into a rotary movement. The rotary movement having been secured, it is passed along to the rear wheel. Now that is simple enough but it is not done quite so simply. The spark has to occur at precisely the right moment. The valves have to open and close with precision so as to permit a new charge to enter and the burned gas to escape. You now have a rough idea of the operation. Let us examine the various parts of the engine and see how they enter into the general scheme.

The Cylinder. The Rudge cylinder is a cast-iron barrel of uniform diameter, whose inner surface or " wall " is smooth as glass. Its exterior is finned so as to trap and circulate cool air, and thereby keep the metal cooler than would otherwise be the case. The inner wall is smooth so as to be a perfect fit with the piston and prevent the escape of gas from the space between the top of the piston and the cylinder head when that gas is under compression.

The Piston. The piston is really a buffer, similarly shaped to the cylinder in which it works. It has to fit the wall of the cylinder so tightly that no gas can escape, and so that a partial vacuum may be formed on its downward stroke. To fit a cylinder with so tight a piston seems to suggest that the piston could not work freely, and since its up and down speed is very considerable indeed, obviously something must be done to secure freedom of movement and also tightness.

The Piston Rings. This is done as follows: The piston has narrow grooves turned on the outside of it. Into these grooves are fitted rings made of springy iron. The rings are cut, so

HOW AN ENGINE WORKS

that they can expand and thereby ensure gas-tightness with the cylinder walls. Thus the piston itself is actually slightly smaller than the inner chamber of the cylinder.

The Connecting-rod. In order that the up and down motion of the piston may be turned into rotary movement, it is hinged at its top to a connecting-rod, which reaches into its hollow interior. The rod is also hinged at its lower end to the crank pin. Thus as the piston moves up and down the connecting-rod turns the crankshaft. The connection between the rod and the piston is called the gudgeon-pin. The crank pin connection is the "big end."

The Flywheel. Having turned our power into a rotary movement, it is now necessary to have some sort of governor, and this introduces the flywheel, whose function it is to secure, by momentive energy, sufficient power to send the piston on the three of its four strokes which are not power strokes. We are now fairly clear as to the manner in which propulsive energy is obtained.

Valve Mechanism. We will now explain how the explosive gas is introduced into the combustion chamber, and how the burnt gas is evicted. We know that the reciprocating, or up and down, action of the piston is translated into a rotary movement at the engine shaft. One side of this shaft is employed, as has been described, for the transmission. On the other side the rotary movement is used for the valve mechanism and the timing of the spark. The Rudge valves—there are two inlet and two exhaust (except on the 250 c.c. models)—are of the overhead type, that is to say, they are contained in the head of the cylinder.

On this side of the crankshaft there is a small pinion or cogwheel which engages with a cam-wheel, which has two cams formed on it. This is known as the two-to-one gear, and it is necessary in order that the valves may move but once during two revolutions of the crankshaft. The cam-wheel, in revolving, lifts a push-rod. This push-rod, moving up and down, actuates a rocker which swivels on its pivot above the cylinder head and the rocker presses the valve down so that there is a clearance between it and its seating in the cylinder.

The cams are so fitted to the cam-wheel that they open the valves at a predetermined period in the engine cycle. First of all there is the suction stroke when the piston is moving down the barrel of the cylinder. It is necessary that the inlet valve should be open during this so that a charge of explosive gas may be drawn in from the inlet pipe leading from the carburettor. The cam is, therefore, pushing the inlet valve push-rod while the piston is descending. When the piston reaches the bottom of its stroke, the cam has passed round, and the strong springs, which are fitted to each valve, have closed the valves on their seatings. The supply of gas is, therefore, cut off. The piston now moves upwards, and compresses the gas at the top of its stroke. At about this time, the spark occurs at the plug points, and fires the compressed gas. The explosion forces down the piston, thus

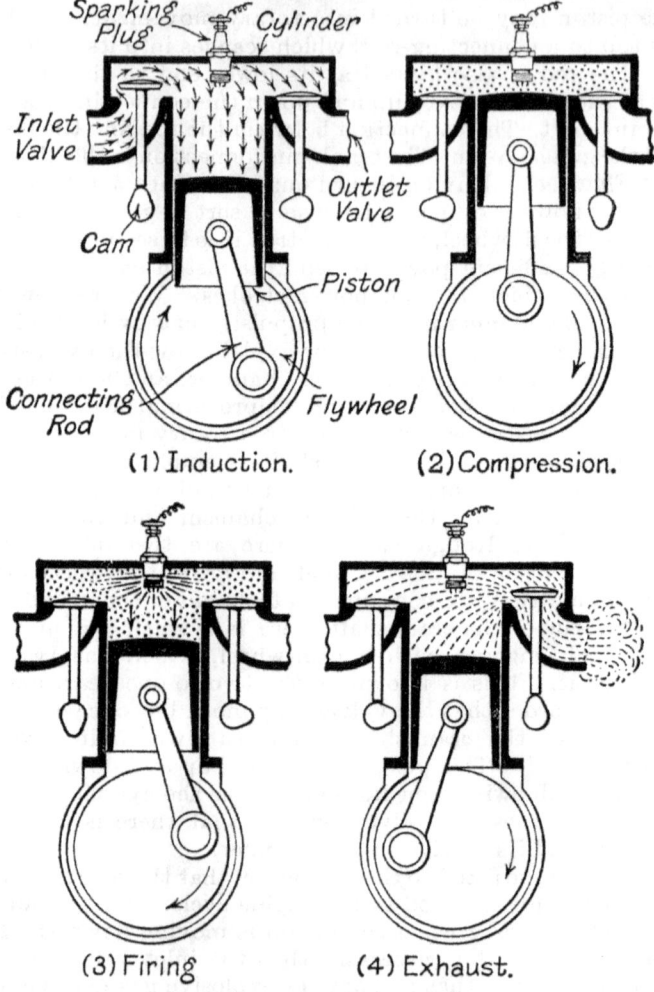

Fig. 16. The Four-stroke Cycle

giving us the one power stroke, which we get in four piston movements. The rotation of the flywheel forces the piston up again on its exhaust or scavenging stroke. As it moves upward so the exhaust valves open in precisely the same fashion as did the inlet

HOW AN ENGINE WORKS

valves. The burnt gas is discharged through the orifices, conducted along the exhaust pipes into the silencer, or expansion box, and therefrom into the atmosphere through the extension pipe. Let us number and particularize our piston strokes.

1. Suction or induction. (The piston is descending and the inlet valve is open.)
2. Compression. (The piston is rising and the explosion or combustion chamber is gas tight with both valves closed.)
3. Explosion, or power stroke. (The piston is descending by force of the explosion, and both valves are still closed.)
4. The exhaust, or scavenging stroke. (The piston is ascending again and sweeping out the burnt gas through the exhaust valve which has opened.)

Before describing in detail the various features of Rudge machines, it is perhaps desirable to tabulate the various models.

1938–9 RANGE OF MODELS

Model	Bore and Stroke (mm.)	Valves	Lubrication	Tyres	Tax
250 c.c. Rapid	62 × 81	2 O.H.V.	Dry Sump	26" × 3·25"	£1 17s. 6d.
250 c.c. Sports	62 × 81	2 O.H.V.	Dry Sump	26" × 3·25"	£1 17s. 6d.
500 c.c. Special	84·5 × 88	4 O.H.V.	Dry Sump	26" × 3·25"	£3 15s.
500 c.c. Sports Special	84·5 × 88	4 O.H.V.	Dry Sump	26" × 3·25"	£3 15s.
500 c.c. Ulster	85 × 88	4 O.H.V.	Dry Sump	27" × 3·0" Front 27" × 3·25" Rear	£3 15s.

All machines are of the single-cylinder type and have the same general characteristics embodying—

Four overhead valves (except on the 250 c.c. models).
Dry sump lubrication.
Aluminium alloy pistons.
Roller bearings for the connecting-rod.
Four-speed gears with foot change.
Interchangeable wheels (except on the 250 c.c. models).
Patent system of proportional coupled brakes.
Steel flywheels.
Oil bath to primary chains.

The policy of the makers in submitting their machines to the drastic tests of road racing and competition, and the success attained, should give owners confidence in the reliability of the design and construction of all machines in the range of models available. The knowledge and experience gained in this manner is applied in full measure to the construction of the touring machines, and the heavy repair bill, consequent upon hard driving, will be avoided in models built on this foundation. Nor will it be found that the refinements demanded by the fastidious driver are omitted from the specification of these machines. As would

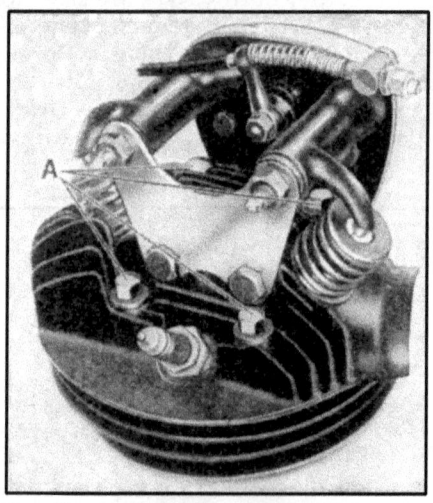

Fig. 16a. The Single-port Two-valve Cylinder Head and Overhead Valve Gear used on the 250 c.c. Rudges

At *A* are shown the four cylinder head fixing bolts. The overhead rocker spindles are not enclosed in an automatically lubricated rocker-box as on the "five hundreds" but are carried by side plates and lubricated by grease nipples as shown

be expected, the capabilities of these machines with regard to high, maximum, and average speeds and general reliability, will not disappoint either the rider who enjoys fast speed work on the open road or the man to whom unfailing reliability under all and every condition is an essential.

The Crankcase. This is of aluminium, split on the vertical centre line, and carries a pair of built-up flywheels and a single roller bearing on the timing side, but, on the driving side, in addition to the roller bearing, there is fitted a ball bearing which supports the driving shaft, close up to the driving sprocket. On the timing side there is an extension below the timing box which carries the plunger of the oil pump, and a communicating passage between the oil pump and the bottom of the crankcase is provided.

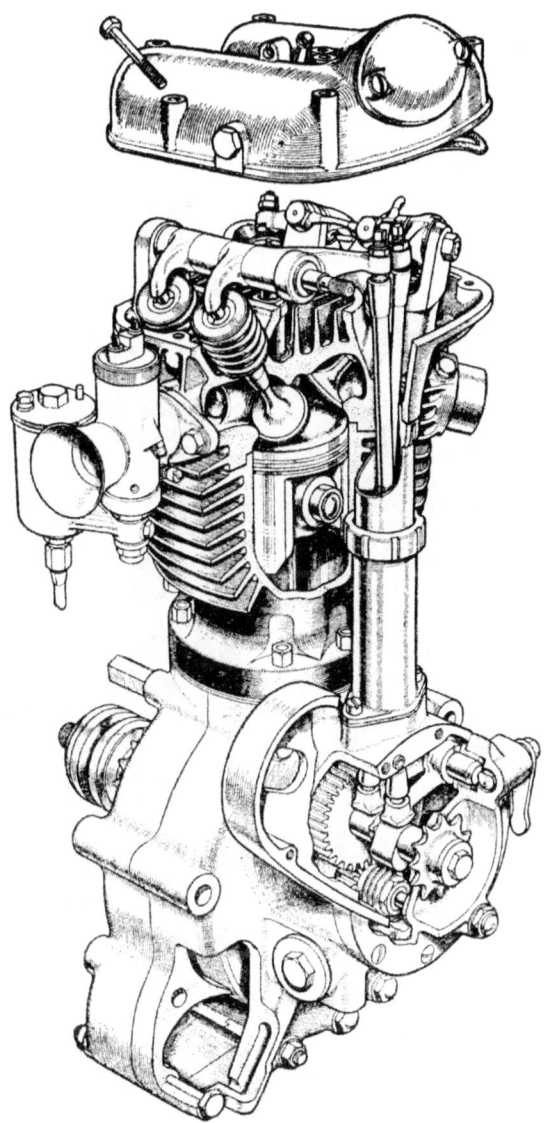

Fig. 17. Partly Sectioned View of Rudge "Ulster" Engine with Rocker-box Cover Removed

This illustration shows the extremely neat enclosure of the four-valve mechanism and push-rods. The overhead rockers are lubricated by a feed from the oil pump and the push-rods are socketed top and bottom, no tappets being provided

(*From "The Motor Cycle"*)

The Flywheels. These are of the built-up type, and a large crankpin, which carries the roller bearings for the connecting-rod, is fitted in parallel holes in both the steel flywheels. The driving

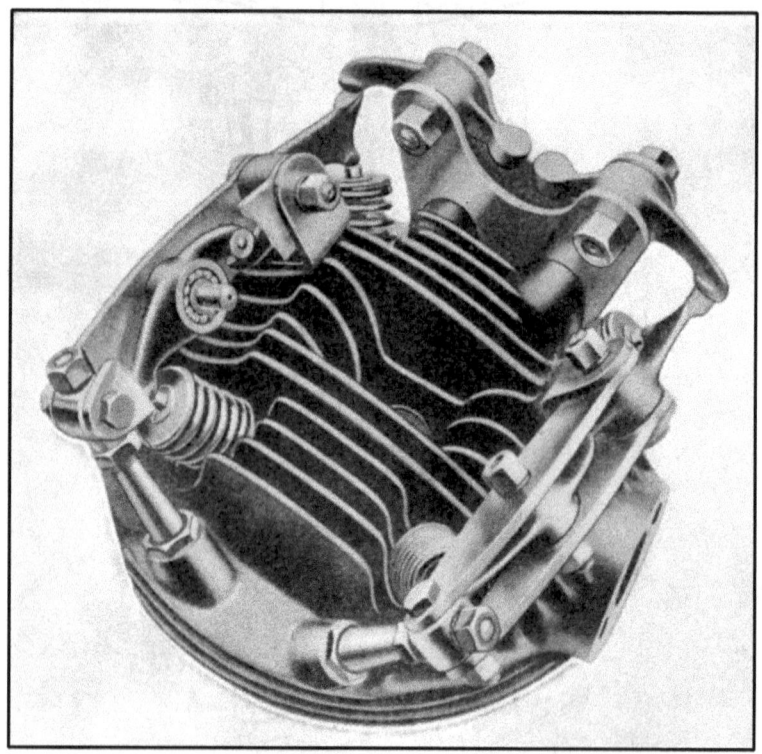

FIG. 18. THE 1935-6 250 C.C. RADIAL VALVE CYLINDER HEAD

shaft and the axle for the timing gear are both fitted in taper holes in the flywheels. The timing pinion fits on a taper end of the axle and is provided with a screwed thread for purposes of withdrawal, and a slot at the end of the pinion engages a corresponding projection on the worm, which drives the oil pump plunger.

The oil pump on all Rudge engines is fitted in the timing case and since it comprises a single double-acting plunger with port action there is practically no likelihood of trouble arising.

The Double-Acting Oil Pump. The small end of the pump draws oil from the oil tank and is provided with ports which feed the greater proportion of oil through the right-hand crankshaft axle to the big-end bearing. This has to pass through a small tell-tale,

HOW AN ENGINE WORKS 39

which, when the pump is operating, moves outwards and is visible to the rider. The remaining oil is fed through two small

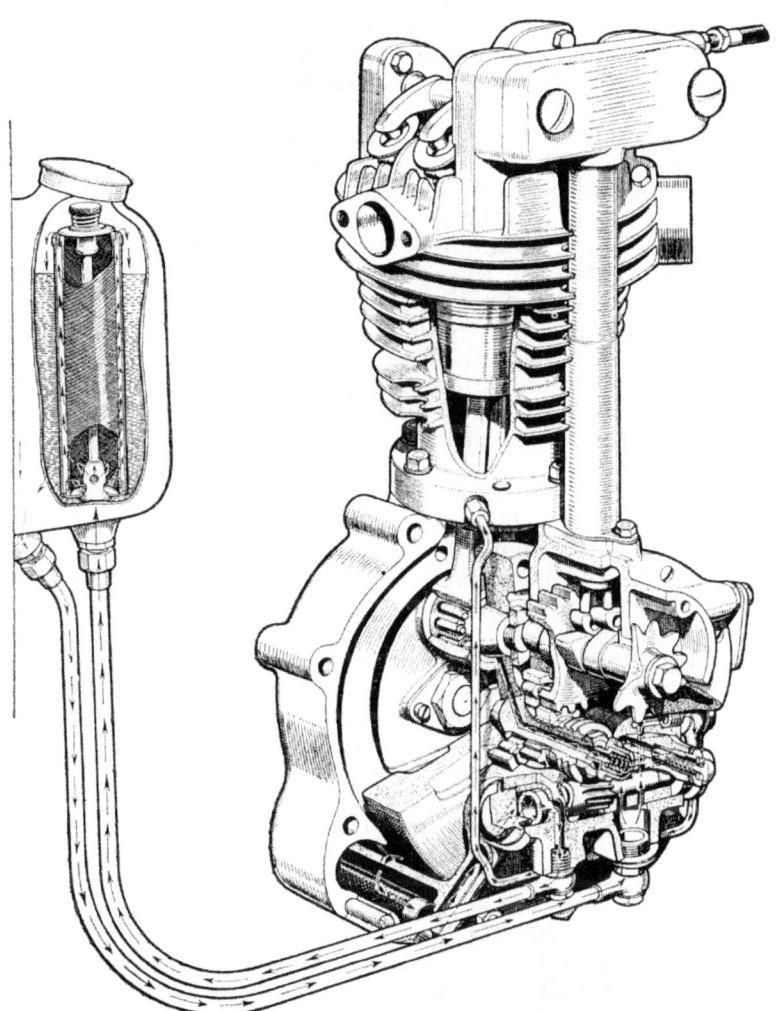

Fig. 18a. Showing the Arrangement of the Dry-sump Lubrication System (1933-6 "Special" Engines)

pipes to the rear of the cylinder and also to the pair of overhead rockers. The large end of the pump draws oil from the sump in the crankcase, where the surplus oil is collected, and forces it back to the oil tank. Here it is forced past a felt type filter, which collects any sediment or metallic particles. This filter, shown in Fig. 18A, is removable through the tank filler cap and should occasionally be cleaned. A spring-loaded valve is fitted to the cap of the filter so that, in the event of the filter becoming choked with sediment, no damage will result to the oil pump. There is very little chance of this occurring, however, since the filter is of very large dimensions. There is also a further gauze filter fitted at the bottom of the oil sump (1933-6), removable from the left-hand side of the crankcase after removing the chain case.

It is thus seen that oil is constantly circulating and all that is left for the rider to watch is that there is oil in the tank. It is good practice to keep the oil tank fairly full, so that the temperature of the oil will not be excessive (see Chapter IV).

Connecting-rod. The rod is of "H" section and fits on roller bearings. The small-end of the connecting-rod carries a large diameter gudgeon-pin, fitted with bronze pads at each end.

Piston. This is of hard aluminium alloy and has two rings, the lower acting as a scraper ring. Small holes through the piston are drilled just below the bottom ring to provide a return path for the oil (on some engines) scraped off the cylinder walls.

Cylinder. The cylinder is of special cast-iron and is fitted with a detachable cylinder head, the holding down bolts for which are inverted and pass through bosses cast on the cylinder. A washer between the cylinder and cylinder head fits on the top face and is centralized by a spigot. The "250" bolts are not inverted.

Timing Gears. The driving pinion, which has ground teeth, engages with similar teeth in the cam gear wheel, which runs at half engine speed. This gear is mounted on the spindle of the cam shaft, two separate cams being used, one to operate the inlet valves, and the other the exhaust valves. A pair of rockers contact with the cams and operate adjustable tappet rods. These, in turn, operate the push-rods, which, at the upper end, contact with the overhead rockers; 1937-9 "500s" have no tappets.

Carburettor. This fitting may be regarded as being the lungs of the motor-cycle. The instrument fitted to all Rudge standard machines is the needle-type Amal, and the operation is as follows: When the piston travels down on the suction stroke, a small volume of air is drawn past a jet or spraying nozzle at a high speed, due to the strong suction and the small aperture through which the air can pass. This air rushes past the top of the jet, draws the petrol out and sprays it into the mixing chamber, and so into the engine. The proportion of petrol and air thus given forms an explosive charge. The supply of mixture is governed by slide valves, which are operated by levers on the handle-bar. These are called the air and throttle levers. The smaller of

HOW AN ENGINE WORKS

the levers is the air lever and is connected by a cable to the air valve in the carburettor. The larger lever, or, alternatively, the twist-grip, operates a slide valve in the carburettor, which, as it increases the petrol supply, also occasions an extra charge of air. Although the throttle lever automatically increases the air supply with the petrol, the air lever permits extra adjustment of the mixture by enriching or weakening it.

When the engine is running slowly at small throttle openings, the speed of the air past the jet is not sufficient to cause the required amount of petrol to issue from the main jet, and consequently a small pilot jet is provided near to the edge of the throttle valve, and the suction on the engine side of the valve draws the petrol through this small jet. Consequently, the pilot jet provides the correct mixture at small throttle openings and compensates for the weaker supply drawn from the main jet at the intermediate throttle positions. At full throttle the pilot jet is practically out of action, the whole of the petrol supply then being induced from the main jet.

The *Float Chamber*, into which the petrol is led from the tank by a pipe, is a simple but ingenious device. When the petrol tap is opened the spirit flows into this chamber, and as the level rises so the float inside the chamber rises with it. As the float rises it takes with it a needle valve, which seals the aperture through which the petrol passes into the chamber when the level of spirit in the chamber is just below the jet outlet. The petrol is now ready for conveyance through the jet, and, as has already been described, it is sucked through this by the air current passing over it.

A possible trouble in the carburettor is that of "flooding," as a result of which petrol escapes from the float chamber and is wasted. This is usually caused by the fact that the needle valve in the float chamber does not properly close the orifice in which it rests. This may be occasioned because the needle is not properly vertical, or because dust or other impurity clogs the orifice and does not allow a proper seating between the pin and the hole. A possible, but not a probable cause, is that the float itself is punctured, so that it will not rise as the petrol flows in. This is to be ascertained by removing the float from the chamber and shaking it to see if any petrol has got into the inside. The needle having become worn or bent would again prevent a proper seating. On the float-chamber lid will be found a small button. This is the "tickler," and is intended for starting purposes only. By its depression the needle is forced from the orifice in which it rests, and petrol flows in at once. But it should not be "tickled" —only depressed, and the pressure should not be maintained for long, otherwise there will be extravagant flooding, and liquid petrol may be forced through the jet and render starting difficult.

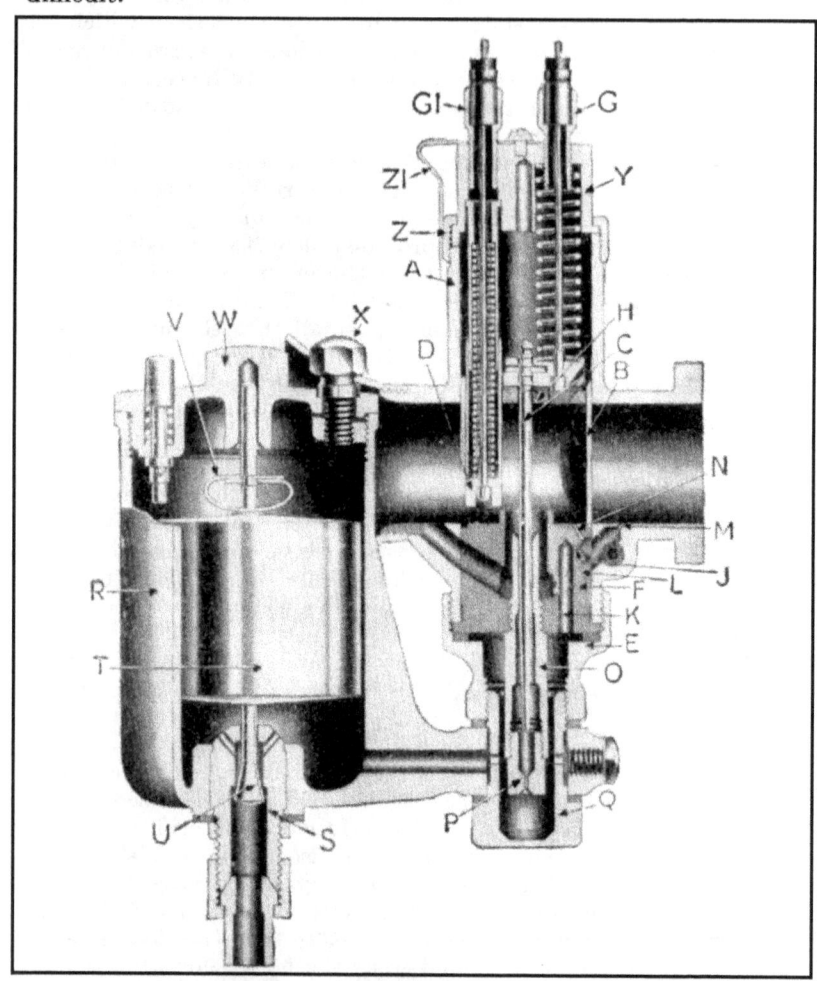

Fig. 19. Sectional View of Semi-automatic Needle Jet, Amal Carburettor

(*Messrs. Amal, Ltd.*)

AMAL SEMI-AUTOMATIC CARBURETTOR

The illustration (Fig. 19) shows a sectional view of the instrument. The body (A) carries a throttle valve (B) and an air slide

HOW AN ENGINE WORKS

(D), both of which are operated by Bowden wires and the return springs shown. On the inside of the mixing chamber is the jet block (F), which is held firmly in position by the union nut (E), with the fibre washer interposed to ensure a petrol-tight joint. Into the jet block is screwed a needle jet (O), into which is screwed a main jet (P). The jet plug (Q) clamps the union joint of the float chamber, so that on removal of the jet plug the main jet and needle jet can be removed. The pilot jet (J) is integral with the jet block and communicates with the main jet supply through passage (K). The adjustable pilot air intake (L) communicates with outlet (M) and by-pass (N). The float chamber body (R), previously mentioned, is supported by the carburettor body, and the petrol feed is connected at the lower part of the float chamber body. Petrol thus rises past the needle valve (U) and causes the hollow float (T) to rise, carrying with it the needle, so that, when the float chamber is filled to the proper level, the needle rises and closes the fuel passage.

The float chamber having filled to its correct level, fuel passes along the passages, through the diagonal holes in the jet plug (Q), when it will be in communication with the main jet (P) and the pilot feed hole (K); the level in the needle and pilot jets being, obviously, the same as that maintained in the float chamber.

Operation. Imagine the throttle valve (B) very slightly open. As the piston descends a partial vacuum is created in the carburettor, causing a rush of air through the pilot air hole (L) and drawing fuel from the pilot jet (J). The mixture of air and fuel is admitted to the engine through the pilot outlet (M). The quantity of mixture capable of being passed by the pilot outlet (M) is insufficient to run the engine. This mixture will not ignite, as there is not sufficient air to combine with the amount of petrol admitted. Consequently, in order to obtain a combustible mixture, throttle valve (B) must be slightly raised, admitting a further supply of air from the main air intake. The farther the throttle valve is opened, the less will be the depression on the outlet (M), but, in turn, a higher depression will be created on the by-pass (N), and the pilot mixture will flow from this passage as well as from the outlet (M). The mixture provided by the pilot and by-pass system is supplemented at approximately one-eighth throttle by fuel from the main jet system, the throttle valve cut-away governing the mixture strength from here to one-quarter throttle. Proceeding up the throttle range, mixture control by the position of the needle takes place from one-quarter to three-quarter throttle, and thereafter the main jet is the only regulation. The air valve (D) has the effect of obstructing the main through-way, and, in consequence, increasing the depression on the main jet, enriching the mixture.

CHAPTER IV
LUBRICATION

THE inexperienced motor-cyclist may take to heart the axiom that oil is cheaper than bearings. When metal surfaces are rubbing together considerable friction and wear must ensue unless a thin film of oil is maintained between the surfaces. The Rudge rider is fortunate in this respect. The oiling system is mechanical and thoroughly reliable. All that the rider need concern himself with is the contents of the oil tank, which is mounted beside the seat-pillar. From this reservoir the engine and all its parts are mechanically fed, and just below the foot of the magneto chaincase is a little plunger or piston, which constitutes a telltale. So long as this plunger is oscillating, the machine, or rather the power unit, is receiving lubricant. The Rudge dry-sump lubrication system has already been described and illustrated.

There are several satisfactory oils which may be used for the Rudge machine, but the rider should use those which are recommended by the makers, viz. Castrol Grand Prix, Shell X–100 SAE 50 (SAE 40 during winter), Mobiloil D (BB during winter), Price's Energol SAE 50, and Essolube 50 (40 during winter). For 1936-9 "Ulster" models Essolube Racer is the correct grade to use.

It is certainly possible to buy oil cheaply when no particular brand is specified, but the actual cost of that oil might be very high if it were not efficient and sufficiently viscous. Bearings are relatively expensive, and badly or insufficiently oiled bearings have to be renewed far more frequently than those which are adequately oiled. If you use Patent Castrol "R" for racing it is essential to drain and clean the oil tank before changing over from a mineral base oil such as Castrol Grand Prix.

The most common mistake made by novices in regard to lubrication is to neglect the actual cycle parts. They forget that, apart from the engine, there is the gear box and the many little bearing surfaces of the frame or cycle parts which require attention. Wherever grease is necessary on the machine itself, there will be found a greaser nipple, and these should be generously lubricated. At frequent intervals the owner should make a detailed "tour" of the machine with a suitable grease-gun, and he should see that the oil goes into the bearings and is not merely contained in the greasers, which may have become clogged. When greasing a shaft continue till grease commences to exude.

LUBRICATION 45

During the oiling "tour" it is an excellent plan to carry an adjustable spanner, wherewith nuts may be tested for tightness. The "oiling-adjusting" inspection of a machine is an important factor in the retention of reliability, and it should be undertaken frequently. A well-lubricated machine, and not merely a well-oiled engine, is essential. The latter obtains almost automatically, because of the dry sump pump system employed on the Rudge machine, but only adequate attention to the bicycle parts will secure the proper lubrication of the machine itself.

ENGINE LUBRICATION

Engine lubrication will be dealt with first, as this is of primary importance. The bearings in the engine work at very high speed and big forces come into play. Moreover, the cylinder and piston get very hot when the engine is running and any neglect in the small attention which the rider has to see to in the matter of engine lubrication quickly brings evil consequences, perhaps of a very serious and expensive nature. The cycle parts are not nearly so severely stressed and the bearings normally run quite cold.

The Engine Oil Supply is not Adjustable. No adjustment is provided either for the main oil supply to the big-end bearing or for the auxiliary supply to the rear of the cylinder (Fig. 18A) and the sole responsibility on the part of the Rudge owner is: (a) to maintain an adequate supply of *suitable* oil in the tank; (b) to check oil circulation after starting up and occasionally while riding; (c) to keep the tank and engine sump filters clean and renew the tank filter occasionally; (d) to keep the pipe connections air-tight.

It is a good plan at long intervals (say every 2,000 miles) to drain the whole of the oil from the tank, clean the tank and filter with petrol, and replenish with entirely fresh oil. Although not essential (owing to the adequate filters used), some riders while decarbonizing like to drain and swill out the crankcase. If this is done care should be taken to remove *all* traces of petrol or paraffin to prevent oil dilution, and before replacing the cylinder some clean oil should be put on the big-end and the flywheels. All surplus oil will quickly be returned to the tank by the oil pump whose return side is of considerably larger capacity than the delivery side.

(a) **Keep Oil Tank at Least Half Full.** This is *exceedingly important* because unless there is a sufficient volume of oil in circulation the temperature of the oil drawn into the engine via the suction pipe will be higher than it should be and the lubricating qualities of the oil will suffer in consequence. As a general rule, maintain the oil tank nearly full by replenishing frequently

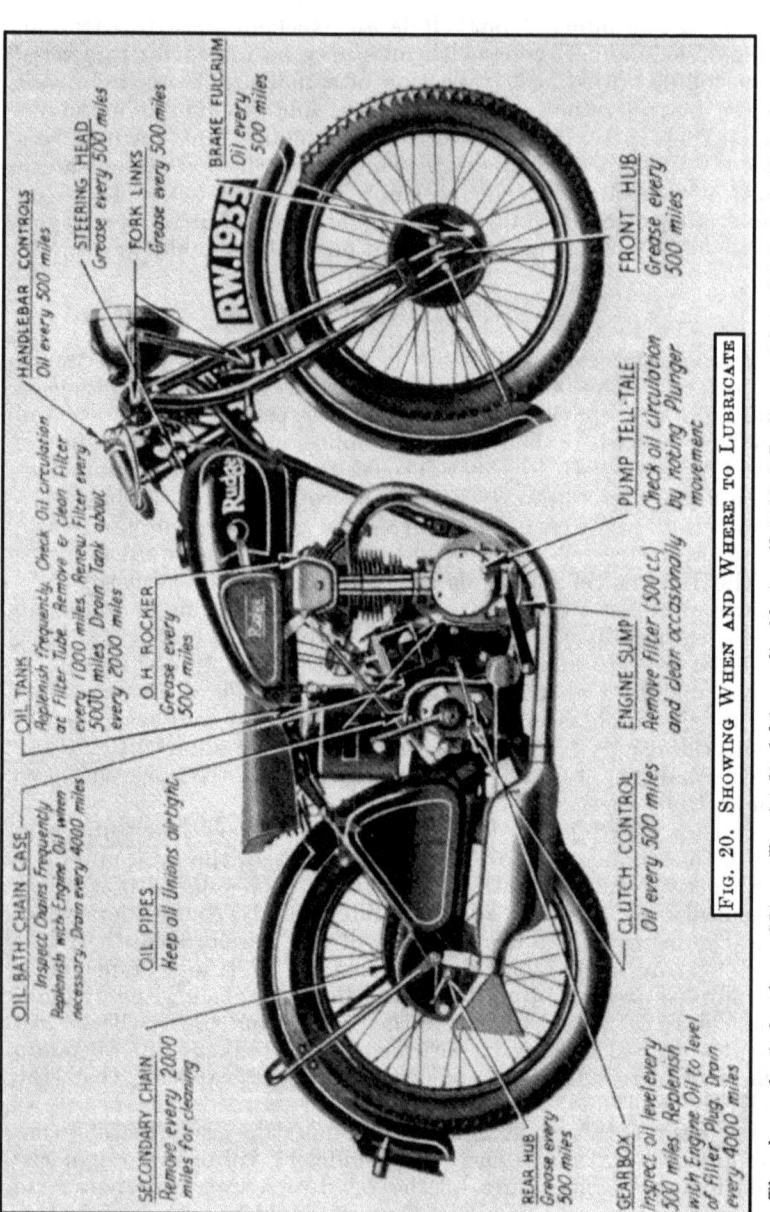

Fig. 20. Showing When and Where to Lubricate

The above chart showing a 250 c.c. Tourist Model is applicable to all 1933–9 Rudge models and is intended to serve as a guide rather than to be followed exactly. On the 1937–9 models a sump filter is not fitted. See also pages 52 and 53.

LUBRICATION

with oil of one of the grades recommended at the beginning of this chapter. Serious damage to the engine and perhaps a bad seizure may arise through allowing the oil to drop appreciably below the half-way level.

On buying a second-hand Rudge it may be found that there is very little oil in the tank. Do not make the fatal mistake of starting up the engine before filling the tank. To be on the safe side it is best before starting up to kick the engine over several times until movement of the tell-tale indicates that the oil is in circulation.

To Check Oil Circulation. After starting up and sometimes while riding you should glance at the oil tell-tale situated just below the magneto chaincase (on the 250 c.c. models there is no chaincase on this side). As may be understood by reference to Fig. 18A, the main oil supply immediately after leaving the delivery side of the pump is in communication with a small passage terminating in a small spring-loaded piston or plunger. Thus, as the oil pressure rises it pushes out this plunger, which moves in or out according to the oil pressure. If this plunger remains in and does not move, stop the engine immediately because it is evidence that the oil is not circulating.

Apart from the tell-tale, there is another and still more positive method of checking the oil circulation and this is to remove the oil tank filler cap and observe whether oil flows out through the holes round the top of the tube which surrounds the felt filter. This flow proves conclusively that the oil is circulating properly, because this oil is being returned to the tank after circulating throughout the engine.

(c) **Clean Tank Filter about every 1,000 Miles.** The gauze-filter incorporated at the rear of the engine sump (1933–6 500 c.c.) should be cleaned occasionally, and the felt tank filter should also be detached about every 1,000 miles and thoroughly cleaned with petrol. Use a brush, if you like, but do not clean the gauze filter with a rag, as fluff may adhere to the filter and subsequently be very difficult to remove. Drain the oil tank every 2,000 miles.

To remove the oil tank filter unscrew the knurled knob situated directly below the filler cap and lift the filter tube and the felt filter right out of the tank. To ensure the circulation of oil, even in the event of the filter becoming completely choked with impurities, a release valve is provided at the top, but it should be mentioned that a choked filter will cause the oil consumption to rise heavily. About every 5,000 miles you should renew the felt filter. To remove the sump filter for cleaning, it is necessary to remove the primary chain case.

(d) **Keep Pipe Unions Tight.** The proper functioning of the Rudge dry-sump lubrication system is dependent upon there being no air leaks in any of the pipe connections. If an air leak occurs in the suction pipe a mixture of air and oil may be circulated, and this would be indicated by the tell-tale ceasing to move or moving very irregularly. If the tell-tale ceases to function, immediately examine the oil return in the tank and if no oil is being passed, tighten up the nuts at both ends of the suction pipe (Fig. 18A). Should this fail to rectify matters, remove the plug at the end of the pump body and while turning the engine over note whether the plunger is operating. If it remains stationary probably the cause of the trouble is a damaged set pin or damaged teeth on the spindle.

Be Careful with Pump Set Pin. In the event of the pump set pin being removed at any time it is vitally important *before* refitting it to see that the cam groove of the pump plunger is in such a position that the set pin can be inserted with its point in the groove without the application of any force on the pin. Failure to take this precaution will almost certainly cause damage, perhaps of a serious kind, to the pump.

Grease Overhead Rockers about every 500 Miles (1933-6). Once every 500 miles, more often if very hard driving is undertaken, you should inject some suitable high melting-point grease with the grease-gun into the grease nipples provided for lubrication of the overhead rockers. These nipples are variously situated on different engines, some being on the rocker end plates, some on the ends of the rocker pins, and some on the rocker-box (where provided). When greasing the overhead rockers do not forget to put a spot of oil on both ends of the push-rods and at the contacting ends of the rockers; 1937-9 engines have automatic lubrication (except 250 c.c. models). See also page 106.

B.T.-H. Magneto Lubrication. The armature ball bearings are packed with grease on assembly and no further attention is necessary until a very big mileage has been covered.

M-L Magneto and Lucas " Maglita " Lubrication. The remarks in the preceding paragraph with regard to the armature bearings apply here also, but in the case of the "Maglita" a convenient oil hole is provided on the contact-breaker side and oil should be applied at this point about every 1,000 miles. On both the M-L magneto (used on earlier Rudges) and the "Maglita" a spot of oil should be put on the steel face cam about every 1,000 miles also.

Lubrication of the Miller Dynamo. Use oil very sparingly here. A supply of lubricant has been placed in the bearings when assembled, and this should prove sufficient for at least 1,000 miles. A small quantity of grease should be pressed into the hole (to be seen in the commutator end bearing casting) every 1,000 miles. Avoid using too much grease and pressure, otherwise the grease may be forced through the bearing, and this

LUBRICATION

may ultimately reach the commutator and cause considerable trouble. Some Miller dynamos have no greaser.

THE CYCLE PARTS

Inspect Gearbox Oil Level every 500 Miles. First see that the machine is standing on level ground. Then remove the filler plug which covers the hole on the right-hand side just below the kick-starter. This hole is designed to serve as an oil level indicator and a summer grade of good engine oil (see page 44) should be poured through the filler plug hole until the gearbox is full to overflowing. Obviously, it is quite impossible to put excessive oil into

Fig. 21. Showing 1933-6 500 c.c. Rudge Oil Bath Chain Case

On the 250 c.c. models a similar design of chain case is used, but as a "Maglita" is fitted behind the engine the shape of the casting is different. Also the filler and level plugs are combined

the gearbox (unless it is tilted) because the oil level is strictly determined by the position of the filler plug hole. On *no* account replenish the gearbox with thick grease, as this may not circulate properly and cause damage to the box. The Rudge gearbox is designed for running with engine oil only. Incidentally, on a reconditioned machine the gearbox does not invariably contain sufficient oil so be very careful to fill up before taking the machine on the road.

About every 4,000 miles the gearbox should be drained, but do not wash it out with paraffin after doing this.

Replenish Oil Bath Chain Case when Necessary. Both the primary transmission and the dynamo or "Maglita" chains on 1933-9 models run completely enclosed and protected in an aluminium oil bath chain case. To ensure oil-tightness between the two halves of the case a cork washer is provided and a floating bush on the clutch shaft allows of the gear box being moved backwards or forwards without interfering with the oil-tightness of the chain case. As in the case of the gearbox, engine oil of one of the grades recommended on page 44 is advised for replenishment of the oil bath which should be done whenever necessary. Provided the chain case screws are kept done up tight, replenishment should seldom be required, but it is wise to examine the condition of the chains frequently. Both chains run at a comparatively high speed and the length of the chains is not big. Proper lubrication is therefore most important if long life of the chains is desired. When in any doubt as to whether the chains are being adequately lubricated, remove both inspection covers (see Fig. 21), and if necessary replenish with engine oil.

1933–6 500 c.c. models have the filler plug situated above the domed shape boss surrounding the engine sprocket. Remove this plug and also the oil level plug which will be found just above the exhaust pipe and pour in oil until it begins to run from the oil level plug hole. Replace the filler plug and *when oil ceases to flow*, the level plug also. It is important not to replenish the oil bath without first removing the level plug, because if the case is overfilled there may be a tendency for clutch slip or drag to occur due to excessive oil clinging to the clutch plates. This tendency, however, is considerably reduced on the 1935–9 models by a clutch improvement.

On the 250 c.c. models there is no separate oil level plug, and engine oil should be poured in through the filler plug hole until no more can be added. In the case of all reconditioned machines drain the chain case after the first 200 miles running and replenish with fresh oil. Subsequently, it should not be necessary to drain the chain case more often than every 4,000 miles when draining the gearbox. Even with complete enclosure, the oil does eventually get slightly contaminated with metal dust from the chain rollers and sprockets.

Lubricating Secondary Chain. This is automatically lubricated by a pipe leading from the crankcase breather and as a rule provides adequate lubrication. Never allow the secondary chain to run dirty, because this chain is not completely enclosed and suffers rapidly if cleanliness is neglected.

From time to time (say about once every 2,000 miles) it is a good plan to remove the secondary chain and immerse it in a bath of paraffin. The chain should be allowed to soak well to ensure all the dirt from the rollers being removed and afterwards hung up to dry. When the chain has been cleaned it is wise to lubricate it before refitting it to the sprockets. The best method of doing this is to soak the chain in a receptacle containing a mixture of hot graphite grease and engine oil, which will permeate all the chain roller bearings. See also page 106.

The Steering Head. Two grease nipples are provided for the ball bearings in the steering head, and the grease gun should be applied to them about once every 500 miles. A medium-bodied grease, such as that used for the wheel hubs, is suitable for the steering head and the other cycle parts. See page 106.

Front Forks. The fork link spindles require periodic lubrication, and the grease gun should be applied to the grease nipples about every 500 miles. Also grease the spring box bush.

Wheel Hubs. Both the front and rear hub ball races should be charged with a medium-bodied, high melting-point grease roughly once every 500 miles. When a sidecar is fitted do not neglect to lubricate the sidecar hub. It is very important to keep the bearings of all wheels thoroughly greased, as they are called upon to carry very heavy stresses. Care should be taken not to overcharge the hubs or grease may be forced into the brake drums, with the result that the brakes lose much of their efficiency. If the hubs and other parts are regularly greased, one depression of the grease gun should be sufficient at each nipple.

Brakes. About every 500 miles go carefully over the whole of the brake mechanism and lubricate with oil the anchor plate cam spindles and the various joints. The pedal shaft should also be slightly lubricated.

The Gear Control. The various joints in the hand or foot gear mechanism should be oiled about every 500 miles. Do not overlook the fulcrum of the gear lever itself and the various joints and pivots. These should be oiled about every 500 miles.

Clutch Lubrication. About every 500 miles the external clutch operation should be oiled, and occasionally the clutch operating plunger should be removed from the hollow mainshaft and greased. It is particularly important that this plunger should be able to slide backwards and forwards with absolute freedom, otherwise it is impossible to maintain an "easy" clutch action. Do not forget to keep the actuating lever well lubricated, particularly at the point where the adjusting screw is in contact with the felt washer covering the plunger.

The Engine Shaft Shock Absorber. In the case of all 1933-9 machines provided with oil bath chain cases the shock absorber is automatically lubricated by the oil in the chain case.

Control Levers. About every 500 miles, or perhaps earlier, lubricate with an oil can the various handlebar control levers and see that the exposed ends of the Bowden cables are also well oiled. It is essential for their smooth working that Bowden controls should be kept well lubricated. If lubrication, as outlined above, is never neglected the Bowden cables will retain their original smoothness, but if once they are allowed to become dry, the only satisfactory method is to remove them from the machine, hang them up and allow oil to trickle down between the inner and outer casing while working the inner cable up and down.

Stand and Saddle Pins. Little lubrication points which count are the central stand pivot pin and the pin securing the peak of the saddle. Apply a spot of oil every 300–500 miles.

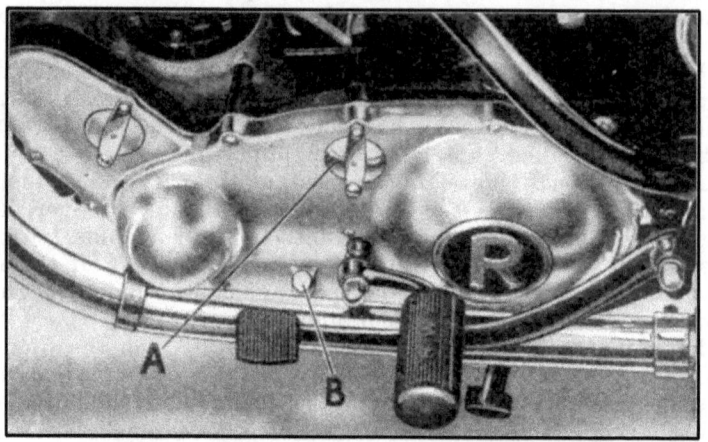

Fig. 22. 1937–9 500 c.c. Oil Bath Chain Case

Oil Bath Chain Case on 1937–9 Models. The oil bath chain case on the 1937–9 "five-hundreds" (Fig. 22) has no filler plug as on earlier models. Instead, the inspection hole with quickly-detachable cover *A* serves for filling purposes, and engine oil (page 44) should be poured into the hole with the level plug *B* removed. Do not replace the level plug until oil ceases to flow. On the 1937–9 250 c.c. models the level plug as hitherto acts as a filler plug also. Over-filling may cause clutch slip (250 c.c.) or oil leakage (500 c.c.).

CHAPTER V
GARAGING AND MAINTENANCE

A CONSIDERABLE number of motor-cycles are stored in public garages, and though there are objections to this, such storage is to be preferred to private but careless housing. If you have a garage attached to your house then you are fortunate, but I do not advocate what might be termed makeshift accommodation.

PERIODICAL ATTENTIONS (1937-9 Models)

Below are summarized the principal attentions required to keep Rudge machines in good running order. These apply to the 1937 models onwards. For a similar summary applicable to 1933-6 models, see page 24. It should be particularly noted that each of the items mentioned below should be dealt with after the first 500 miles in the case of a reconditioned machine.

Every 500 Miles—
REPLENISH   Oil tank to correct level.
            Gearbox to level plug hole.
CHECK   Overhead rocker adjustments.
GREASE   Bearings provided with grease nipples.
OIL   Gear control.
            Control cables.
            Clutch operating screw covered by felt washer.
            Magneto and dynamo (see page 48).

Every 1,000 Miles—
CHECK   Brake adjustment.
            Clutch adjustment.
            Chain adjustment (primary, rear, dynamo, magneto).
            Oil level in chain case.

Every 2,000 Miles—
DRAIN   Oil tank, clean filter and replenish with fresh oil.
            Tighten oil unions.

Every 4,000 Miles—
DRAIN   Chain case and gearbox and replenish with fresh oil.
CHECK   Tightness of engine and frame bolts.
            Contact-breaker gap.
            Plug point gap.
            Soundness of electrical connections.
            Steering head adjustment.

CLEAN	Carburettor.
	Petrol filter in tank.
	Commutator of dynamo.
	Inside of brake drums (if braking poor).
GREASE	Speedometer gearbox.

Weekly—

CHECK	Tyre pressures with reliable gauge.
CLEAN	Machine.

Monthly—

CHECK	Battery acid level.

Care of Tyres. Modern tyres such as Dunlop, Avon, and Goodyear are excellent, but to obtain long life from the tyres and good performance from the machine it is essential to maintain the correct tyre pressures which are given below for the various models. For pillion riding it is advisable to increase the pressure for the rear tyre by about 5 lb. per sq. in. Make a practice of regularly checking the pressures with a pressure gauge. Comprehensive advice on the care of tyres will be found on pages 69 to 74.

RECOMMENDED INFLATION PRESSURES (DUNLOP "UNIVERSAL")
(*In lb. per sq. in.*)

1936-9 Rudge Model	Front Solo	Rear Solo	Rear Sidecar	Sidecar Wheel
250 c.c. "Rapid" (26 × 3·25)*	16	20	—	—
250 c.c. "Sports" (26 × 3·25)	16	20	—	—
500 c.c. "Special" (26 × 3·25)	20	22	28	16
500 c.c. "Sports Special" (26 × 3·25)	20	22	28	16
500 c.c. "Ulster" (27 × 3, F. 27 × 3·25, R)	26	22	28	16

VARIOUS ADJUSTMENTS (1937-9)

Valve Clearances. To ensure absence of mechanical clatter, flexibility of running, and a good all-round engine performance, the valve clearances must be kept correctly adjusted, and the adjustment should be checked after a few hundred miles on a reconditioned engine and subsequently at intervals of about 500 miles. Rudge and other high efficiency engines are very sensitive

---

* 26 × 3·25 in. tyres according to the new description recently adopted are called 3·25 × 19 in. Similarly 27 × 3 in. and 27 × 3·25 in. are called 3·00 × 21 in. and 3·25 × 20 in. respectively.

in regard to the valve clearances. All Rudge engines should have the clearances checked with the engine absolutely cold.

500 c.c. O.H. Rocker Adjustment. No tappets are provided on the 1937–9 500 c.c. engines and, as may be seen in Fig. 17, the two long push-rods directly engage both the overhead rockers and cam followers. To check the valve clearances, remove the inspection cover provided on the right-hand side of the cover of the rocker-box (which is integral with the cylinder head). Then rotate the engine gently until the piston is on the top of the compression stroke and the cam followers are resting on the cam base circles. Now feel each push-rod. If the valve clearances are correct, it should be just possible to rotate the inlet push-rod with the fingers and in the case of the exhaust push-rod there should be just the slightest up-and-down play perceptible (0·004 in.) with, of course, the engine **cold**.

If the valve clearances are found too small or excessive, they should be corrected by means of the adjuster provided on each overhead rocker arm. Loosen the lock-nut *A* (Fig. 23) and then rotate the adjuster *B* with a spanner applied to its squared end in the necessary direction. Finally retighten the lock-nut, being careful while doing this not to allow the adjuster to move. Then again check the clearances. See also page 87.

250 c.c. Tappet Adjustment. Although tappets have been dispensed with on the 500 c.c. engines, they are still fitted on the 250 c.c. two-valve engines. In this case the adjustment should be made as described on page 88 for the pre-1937 "Special" engine and similar clearances (with the engine **cold**) should be given, that is, the inlet push-rod should be just free to rotate (no clearance) while there should be a clearance of 0·004 in. between the exhaust valve and overhead rocker. Before making an adjustment it is, of course, necessary to telescope the push-rod cover tube, and if difficulty is experienced in adjusting the exhaust tappet (see Fig. 38), the inlet push-rod should be removed by levering up the O.H. rocker with a screwdriver (see page 90).

The Exhaust Valve Lifter. When adjusting the valve clearances, and at all other times, it is important to maintain some backlash in the exhaust valve lifter control. The handlebar lever should not begin to lift the exhaust valve off its seat until the lever has moved about one-third of its travel. On 500 c.c. engines the exhaust valve lifter is incorporated behind the push-rods in the rocker-box cover (Fig. 23), and on 250 c.c. engines it is located behind the off-side rocker plate. The control cable adjuster is situated near the handlebar end of the cable (not at the side of the rocker-box as on previous 500 c.c. engines) and after loosening the lock-nut the cable stop should be screwed in or out the necessary amount. It is important that the **exhaust lifter** cam should never make contact with the exhaust overhead rocker while the engine is running.

To Adjust Clutch Operation. To prevent clutch slip there must always be a little free movement at the handlebar clutch lever,

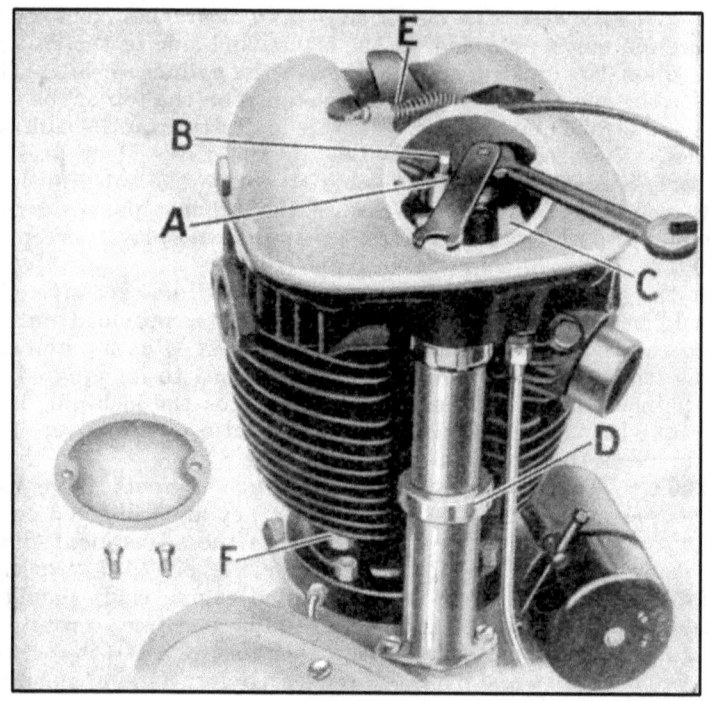

FIG. 23. O.H. ROCKER ADJUSTMENT ON 1937-9 500 C.C. ENGINES

A = Adjuster lock-nut
B = Adjuster
C = Fulcrum for levering up rocker
D = Push-rod cover gland nut
E = Spider bolt
F = Cylinder head nut (inverted)

and in the event of there being no backlash the adjuster lock-nut D (Fig. 6) should be loosened and an adjustment made with the clutch adjuster screw as described on page 90. Lubrication of the clutch operation ensures a smooth action and the advice given on page 51 should be followed.

Removal of Gearbox Apron. A most effective and neat gearbox apron extending well forward below the magneto chain case is fitted on all Rudges. Its removal is a matter of a few minutes only. Remove the footrest crank on the off-side and then

GARAGING AND MAINTENANCE

unscrew the three fixing screws provided on the 500 c.c. models or the single screw on the 250 c.c. models.

Adjustment of Brakes. As hitherto, the rear brake pedal is situated on the off-side on the 250 c.c. models, but on the 500 c.c.

FIG. 24. SHOWING THE IMPROVED REAR BRAKE ON THE 500 C.C. MODELS AND METHOD OF ADJUSTMENT

A = Rear spindle nut
B = Brake anchor bolt
C = Hexagon nut
D = Mudguard bolt
E = Mudguard stay fixing nut
F = Brake adjuster nut

models it has been transferred from the off-side to the near-side. Both front and rear brakes are proportionally coupled and have finger adjustment.

To get the full benefit from the powerful Rudge brakes they must be kept properly lubricated (page 51) and adjusted. To check the adujstment, support the machine so that both wheels are clear of the ground and note if both wheels spin freely when the brake pedal is right home against its stop. Then see if both brakes begin to operate *together* when the rear pedal is depressed ½ in. to 1 in. Some Rudge owners prefer to adjust the brakes so that the front one begins to operate well ahead of the rear, but most prefer a simultaneous action. This does not give maximum retardation with the pedal only, but they use the hand lever also. To ensure correct front and rear leverages the cable connecting the hand lever to the front brake is fitted closer to the brake

Fig. 25. Adjustments for the Front Brake and Steering Head

A = Finger adjusting nut (front brake)
D = Lock-nut for E
E = Adjusting nut (steering head)

GARAGING AND MAINTENANCE

fulcrum than the cable from the brake pedal. The finger adjustments for the rear and front brakes are clearly shown in Figs. 24 and 25 respectively. In the former case there is a large plated nut F (Fig. 24) at the end of the rear brake rod, and in the latter case a similar nut A (Fig. 25) on the off-side of the front forks. A second nut on the forks enables the connecting cable to be lengthened or shortened as required. There are no lock-nuts except on the front forks of the 250 c.c. models.

Removal of Brake Shoes. Should it become necessary to remove the brake shoes in order to clean or renew the linings, this can be done quite readily. In the case of the front brake shoes, it is only necessary to remove the front wheel (see below), when the shoes are instantly accessible. In the case of the rear shoes, proceed to remove the rear wheel (see below) and then unscrew nut C (Fig. 24) and the brake anchor bolt B, push the drum forward to allow the chain to be taken off and then withdraw the complete assembly and remove the shoes.

To Adjust Wheel Bearings. Removal of the front wheel is not necessitated and the bearings should be adjusted as described on pages 91–2 for the 1933–6 models. When the lock-nut on the near-side is firmly retightened it should be possible to feel at the rim a slight trace of play in the bearings. This play is essential, otherwise undue wear of the bearings may occur.

On the 250 c.c. models ball bearings are used for both wheels and the adjustment for the rear one is the same as for the front. The 500 c.c. models, however, have taper roller bearings to carry the rear hub. These bearings are adjusted by means of two nuts on the off-side of the hollow spindle. Adjustment is preferably carried out with the wheel removed from the fork ends. First slacken the lock-nut E (Fig. 26) while preventing the adjusting nut D from rotating. Then if excessive play exists, rotate the adjusting nut *clockwise*. When doing this the hollow spindle must be prevented from rotating. Afterwards retighten the lock-nut E. To avoid over-tightening the bearings it is best to leave slight end play which should be felt at the rim when reassembly, including the spindle nut, is completed. Provided the bearings are kept properly adjusted and occasionally greased (see page 51), they should last as long as the machine.

To Remove Front Wheel. All 500 c.c. models have interchangeable and quickly detachable front wheels and the instructions given on page 92 are applicable. The 250 c.c. models have, of course, no knock-out spindle and the front brake must be disconnected and the complete wheel assembly removed after disconnecting the speedometer cable, removing the brake anchor pin, disconnecting the brake cables, and loosening the spindle nuts.

Removing Rear Wheel. First of all remove the detachable rear mudguard (Fig. 26) as described on page 92 by unscrewing the finger-operated mudguard bolts *D* (Fig. 24) and slackening the nuts *E* which secure the mudguard stays to the rear forks. These nuts on the 250 c.c. models must be completely removed. After

FIG. 26. REAR WHEEL REMOVAL AND BEARING ADJUSTMENT (INSET) ON THE 500 C.C. MODELS

A = Hub bolts
B = Distance piece
C = Spindle head
D = Bearing adjusting nut
E = Lock-nut

disconnecting the lighting wire at the detachable plug, the whole of the mudguard can be withdrawn.

Having removed the mudguard, proceed as follows. On 250 c.c. models follow the instructions given in the paragraph (last but one) on page 92. In the case of 500 c.c. models the three bolts *A* (Fig. 26) should be removed by inserting a box spanner through

GARAGING AND MAINTENANCE 61

the holes in the hub flange opposite. Then unscrew the spindle nut A (Fig. 24) and withdraw the spindle from the tommy-bar end. Knock out the small distance piece B (Fig. 26) and finally ease the wheel out of peg engagement sideways until it comes away from the rear forks. Removal of the wheel on 500 c.c. models does not affect either the chain or brake adjustment. When refitting the quickly detachable wheel, lift it so that the fixed sleeve enters the hollow spindle and turn the wheel until it is possible to engage the pegs. Next replace the distance piece and push the wheel spindle home, tightening up with the nut. The three wheel bolts should be finally refitted and very firmly retightened with the box spanner. After a short spell on the road check over the tightness of these bolts and also the spindle nut.

It should be noted that on some "Ulster" models supplied to special order the drive is through six pegs. Thus there are no bolts and removal of the wheel requires only removal of the spindle and distance piece.

Adjusting Primary Chain. Place the machine on its stand, put the foot gear-change lever in "neutral" and note when turning the engine gently over whether there is a total up-and-down movement mid-way between the sprockets of $\frac{3}{8}$ in. to $\frac{1}{2}$ in. The tension of the chain should be tested with a finger inserted through the inspection cover hole and with the chain in its taughtest position. If adjustment is necessary proceed exactly as described on page 92. Moving the gearbox in order to retension the chain usually upsets the gear control and the adjustment of the foot pedal connecting link should be attended to.

Adjusting Secondary Chain. With the machine jacked up in "neutral," turn the rear wheel backwards and note if, with the chain in the tautest position, there is $\frac{1}{2}$ in. to $\frac{3}{4}$ in. total up-and-down movement mid-way between the sprockets. Excessive play should at once be taken up. On all the 500 c.c. machines there is a cam adjustment which renders it impossible to upset wheel alignment, but this does not apply to the 250 c.c. Rudges where adjustment should be made as described on page 93.

To retension the secondary chain on 500 c.c. models slacken the rear spindle nut A (Fig. 24), large hexagon nut C, and brake anchor bolt B on the near-side of the machine and then rotate the spindle *anti-clockwise* to tighten the chain. After the correct chain tension has been obtained, retighten the sleeve nut, wheel spindle, and brake anchor bolt in this sequence. If the brake adjustment has been disturbed, readjust (see page 57).

Magneto or "Maglita" Chain Adjustment. The instructions given at the bottom of page 94 apply to later Rudge models. As the chain is enclosed and lubricated, adjustment is seldom needed.

The Dynamo Chain. The dynamo armature is eccentrically housed and the chain may be retensioned by turning the dynamo as described on page 94.

Adjustment of Steering Head and Forks. There should be no play in the steering head or fork shackles. Play in the shackles calls for renewal of the shackle bushes but steering head play can be removed by means of the adjusting nut E (Fig. 25) and lock-nut D. The correct method of testing for play and adjusting the steering head is clearly described on page 95. Should there be only *end* play in the fork shackles, this may be removed as also described on page 95.

The Carburettor and Ignition System. Advice on the maintenance and adjustment of the carburettor, plug, and contact-breaker will be found on pages 74 to 80. It is generally unwise to interfere with the carburettor beyond experimenting with the pilot jet adjustment. The correct contact-breaker gap is 0·012 in.

HOW TO DECARBONIZE (1937-9 500 c.c. ENGINES)

Decarbonizing, usually needed every 2,000–3,000 miles, should be done if the engine shows signs of "pinking" due to carbon deposits. Usually the deposits after 2,500 miles are not very heavy and if the engine is running quite well it is sufficient to remove the cylinder head only, not troubling about the barrel. Removal of the piston is, however, advised every alternate decarbonizing when the valves should also be removed and ground-in. In the case of a renovated engine the valves should be ground-in the first time the engine is decarbonized. On Rudge engines it is not necessary to disturb the petrol tank or to dismantle the overhead valve gear, but the push-rods must, of course, be removed.

Preliminary Dismantling. First of all remove the carburettor, exhaust pipes (the finned rings are secured by set screws: the set screws in exhaust ports need not be touched), take off the high tension lead, and disconnect the exhaust valve lifter cable.

Remove the rocker-box inspection cover and lever up the overhead rockers to permit the tubular push-rods to be withdrawn from the recesses in the cam followers and dropped down the push-rod tube. Two small bosses on the inside wall of the cover will be seen when the inspection cap is removed which will facilitate levering up the rockers with a screwdriver C (Fig. 23). The exhaust push-rod should be removed first. Slacken the gland nut in the middle of the tappet tube D (Fig. 23) by means of the "C" spanner in the kit, unscrew the top half out of the head, take out the screws holding the bottom half to the crankcase and detach the oil feed pipe to the cylinder head.

GARAGING AND MAINTENANCE

Removing Cylinder Head. Undo the holding down nuts F (Fig. 23) and unscrew the cylinder head bolts by means of the hexagon fully revealed when the nuts are removed. The head may now be lifted off without disturbing the tank or saddle. If tight, a light tap on the underside of the exhaust ports with a mallet will suffice to loosen the head. When push-rods and tubes are removed, plug up the hole in the crankcase with a cork or rag.

Decarbonizing Piston. Remove all traces of carbon from the top of the piston with a blunt screwdriver (see page 99), taking great care not to scratch the aluminium surface deeply. Afterwards blow away all loose particles of carbon which may be trapped between the cylinder and top piston ring land. Then clean the piston crown with a rag moistened in paraffin. Next deal with the cylinder head and rocker-box.

Dealing with the Cylinder Head. Take out the sparking plug, plug the tapped hole in the tray which carries the top push-rod tube, and thoroughly clean and wash the combustion chamber.

Then turn the head over and undo the central bolt E (Fig. 23) passing through the spider holding the aluminium cover. Lift the left-hand side of the cover first from the head to disengage the valve lifter when it can be withdrawn to expose the rockers and valves. Take great care of the joint washer, on the soundness of which depends freedom from oil leakage.

Thoroughly clean the cylinder head tray, and aluminium cover with a petrol-soaked rag. Move each overhead rocker into engagement with the valves, and verify that both valves will open together. If not, file the stem of the longer valve with a very smooth file until this condition is obtained. After tightening up the oil pipe nuts if necessary replace the washer and cover. The right-hand side of the cover should be placed on the head first and the cover slipped sideways to ensure the valve lifter passing underneath the exhaust rocker arm when the left-hand side may be lowered on the head. The spider should be locked down firmly, but excessive force is unnecessary.

Grinding-in the Valves. The removal of the valve springs is facilitated by placing a block of wood inside the head to hold the valves on their seats while the outer collars are depressed by a suitably shaped steel strip to permit removal of the split collets. The Rudge spares stockists can supply a very cheap tool for this purpose suitable for all Rudge heads. The use of this tool is clearly illustrated in Fig. 27.

In the case of the "Ulster" engine it is necessary first to remove the exhaust rockers from their supports by unscrewing the nuts and withdrawing the fulcrum pins. Keep the bronze bushes with their correct rockers and they will not require attention. The tool mentioned in the preceding paragraph enables the springs to be depressed by levering on the spring collar with the short forked end. Use any convenient bolt passed through the rocker support boss as a pivot.

As the valves and springs, seats and collets are removed, place them on a bench in such a manner that they will be replaced in the same positions. The exhaust valve springs may have closed

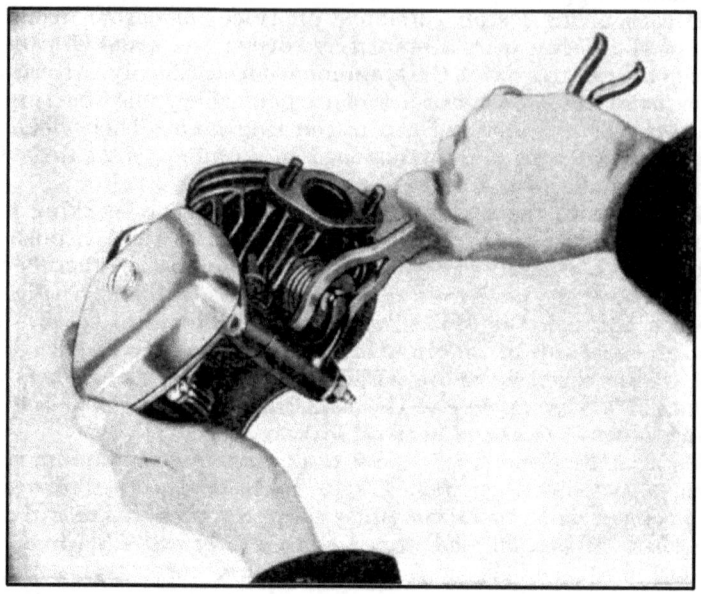

Fig. 27. Compressing Valve Spring on 250 c.c. Head with Rudge Tool

due to heat, but unless they are more than $\frac{1}{8}$ in. shorter, new ones are not necessary.

Clean the valves and if necessary grind them in with a good quality fine grinding paste and oil as described on page 99. Wash all components completely free of dirt and grinding paste, lubricate the valve stems, and reassemble. Attend to the valve clearances as previously described, lubricate all contacting surfaces so that they do not run dry when the engine is first started up, and replace the cover.

Removing the Cylinder and Piston. The cylinder is secured to the crankcase by six nuts at its base. Remove these, detach the oil feed pipe, push the piston to the bottom of its stroke and lift off the cylinder. Mark the piston on one side so that it will be replaced the correct way round, and push out the gudgeon-pin.

GARAGING AND MAINTENANCE

If rather tight, hold the piston for two or three minutes between the palms of the hands, which will loosen the pin. Very carefully remove (see page 97) the rings which must eventually go back into the same grooves. Clean the carbon from the top of the crown, out of the grooves, and from the underside of the crown, if any. Wash well in petrol, dry, and smear liberally with oil.

Clean the carbon from the back of the rings, lubricate them, and replace. If the engine has covered a big mileage, check the ring gaps by means of feelers, after fitting the rings squarely in the cylinder bore, before putting the rings back on the piston. If the gap exceeds 0·025 in. on 500 c.c. models, and 0·020 in. on 250 c.c. models, rings should be renewed. Also if the free gap when not fitted in the bore is less than ¼ in., they should be renewed as the pressure on the walls is insufficient. The correct gap is 0·010 in.

Scrape away the band of carbon at the top of the cylinder, clean thoroughly, and oil liberally.

Reassembling Engine. Replace the piston the correct way round and push in the gudgeon-pin. Renew, if necessary, paper washers between the crankcase and cylinder base, between compression plate and crankcase, and compression plate and cylinder, where the former is fitted. Be most careful to ensure that the piston rings are not broken or strained in refitting the cylinder. Tighten down the cylinder evenly and thoroughly. The two halves of the push-rod tube are telescoped together with the gland nut *loosely* screwed on and placed on the case but not secured thereto. The push-rods are passed through the tube and past the cam to the bottom of the case, the engine having been rotated to bring the exhaust lobe in a forward position, i.e. position of exhaust valve opening. Now replace the cylinder head, verifying that the joint faces are quite clean and the copper washer undamaged. Screw up the bolts and tighten evenly and thoroughly. It is advisable finally to tighten bolts diagonally.

Lift up the push-rods until they both project through the tapped hole in the cylinder head tray; then, dealing with the exhaust push-rod first, insert its bottom end in the cup in the internal rocker and lever up the overhead rocker until the top end of the rod can engage with the spherical end of the adjuster. This operation will be facilitated if the adjuster is first screwed up as far as possible to reduce the amount the rocker must be lifted.

It should be observed that on "Ulster" engines the exhaust push-rod is approximately $\frac{1}{16}$ in. longer than the inlet, and care must be taken to ensure it is fitted in the proper position.

After fitting the inlet push-rod in a similar fashion, screw the top push-rod tube into the cylinder head by means of the "C" spanner in the kit and tighten securely against the copper asbestos washer. Refit the screws holding the bottom push-rod tube to the crankcase and tighten the middle gland nut against its rubber ring. This ring is of special oil and heat resisting rubber—ordinary rubber rings are useless as replacements.

The rocker clearance is adjusted by means of the adjusters accessible through the inspection hole in the cylinder head cover. No clearance on the inlet side and just perceptible clearance on the exhaust side is correct with a cold engine. This adjustment should be checked after a hundred miles or so have been covered

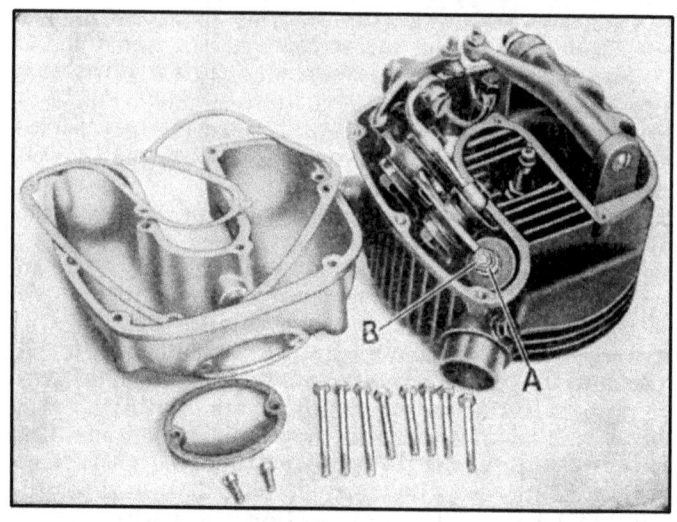

FIG. 28. THE "ULSTER" CYLINDER HEAD AND VALVE GEAR SHOWING EXTRA ROCKER ADJUSTMENT
A = Lock-nut $\quad B$ = Adjuster

subsequent to the overhaul and after retightening cylinder head. The inspection cover, carburettor, silencing system, exhaust lifter cable, and sparking plug remain to be replaced and the machine is again ready for the road.

Similar instructions for decarbonizing the "Ulster" head apply except that the cover is secured to the head by a number of hexagon-headed screws instead of a spider and central bolt, and there is an additional adjuster in the left-hand exhaust rocker to provide a means of obtaining simultaneous contact of the rockers on both exhaust valves. Loosen the lock-nut A (Fig. 28) and rotate the adjuster B until *after* retightening the lock-nut it is possible to place a 0·002 in. feeler between the right-hand rocker and valve when the former is pressed downward to give contact between the left-hand rocker and its valve. It is important that the lock-nut should be thoroughly tightened and that the

GARAGING AND MAINTENANCE

check on clearance should be made subsequently. Wear on this remote rocker is negligible and further attention will be unnecessary until the next overhaul.

DECARBONIZING (1937-9 250 c.c. ENGINES)

The instructions given in the preceding pages are generally applicable to the 250 c.c. engine, but certain constructional differences necessitate an altered procedure which will now be outlined.

Start by removing the carburettor, exhaust pipe, overhead rocker cover and sparking plug. Lever up the rockers and take out the push-rods. The cylinder head is secured to the cylinder by four bolts which are screwed into tapped holes in the latter. When these bolts are unscrewed, the head may be lifted off. They cannot be entirely withdrawn unless the rocker gear is removed, but complete withdrawal is not necessary to enable the head to be detached.

Removing Cylinder. The oil feed pipe must be released without bending it more than necessary, and the tappet tubes should be removed.

Inspecting Timing Gear. This is readily accessible by taking out the screws and withdrawing the timing cover, the ignition drive being on the other side of the machine. Leave the tappets in their guides, and they will keep the cam-wheel in position, which it is unnecessary as a rule to disturb. Inspect, however, the cam followers and the teeth on the pump shaft—the latter by rotating the engine.

Should it be necessary to remove the cam-wheel, undo the nut on the engine shaft, and take off the worm, leaving the pinion in position on its taper. This latter can only be removed with a special extractor.

Reassembling. This is in the main a self-evident proceeding in the reverse order. Be liberal with oil on the piston, timing gear, and valve stems and with grease on the rocker gear. Renew any damaged paper washers and thoroughly tighten all bolts.

DISMANTLING RUDGE ENGINES (1937-9)

More Complete Engine Overhaul. Dismantling of the engine to a greater extent than already described is unlikely to be necessary during the first two seasons of normal running, provided the oil has been regularly changed, and valve clearance adjustment is not neglected.

Inspection of the timing gear can be effected in the following manner. Remove the magneto chain cover, and dismantle the magneto drive. Undo the timing cover screws and withdraw the cover, taking care that the cam-wheel does not follow the cover, thus disturbing the valve timing. The cam followers may be taken out for examination, but the cam-wheel should not be disturbed unnecessarily. If it is to be removed, mark the meshing teeth on half-time pinion and cam-wheel so that the correct valve timing will be obtained on reassembly without trouble. By rotating the engine a few revolutions the condition of the teeth on the oil pump plunger can be observed. Should there be any considerable wear, a replacement is desirable because obviously a failure of a tooth involves a failure of the whole lubricating system. The plunger may be removed by taking out the set screw B (Fig. 6) and both oil pump plugs C (Fig. 6), and pushing the plunger out of the rear end.

Timing the Valves. If the half-time pinion has not been removed, it is merely necessary to replace the cam-wheel so that the marks correspond. Otherwise secure the cylinder head without valve cover or push-rod tubes temporarily by two bolts to the cylinder, fit the cam-wheel, exhaust rocker and exhaust push-rod, and adjust the rocker clearance to 0·020 in. It should be noted that this large clearance is only used for convenience and accuracy in timing the valves and should be adjusted up when the engine is finally erected.

Now rotate the cam in an anti-clockwise direction until the exhaust push-rod is just tight, rotate the engine until the piston position corresponds with the timing for the exhaust valve opening, given on this page, the position of the piston being measured by a rod fitted through the hole in the centre of the cylinder head. Next insert the small timing pinion. The pump worm is then fitted so that the tenon engages the slot in the pinion. When this is done, a firm tap with a hammer at the end of a box spanner should be given and this will cause the pinion to bind on the taper so as not to rotate when the pinion nut is tightened up.

VALVE AND IGNITION TIMING FOR 1937-9 ENGINES

Valve Action, etc.	250 c.c. "Rapid"	250 c.c. "Sports"	500 c.c. "Special" and "Sports Special"	500 c.c. "Ulster"
Inlet opens before T.D.C.	0·2 mm.	8·0 mm.	0·2 mm.	10·0 mm.
Inlet closes after B.D.C.	8·0 mm.	13·2 mm.	8·4 mm.	13·0 mm.
Exhaust opens before B.D.C.	13·4 mm.	13·2 mm.	14·4 mm.	16·0 mm.
Exhaust closes after T.D.C.	2·2 mm.	8·0 mm.	2·4 mm.	10·0 mm.
Magneto advance before T.D.C.	12-14 mm.	12-14 mm.	12-14 mm.	12-14 mm.
Tappet clearance when timing valve	0·025 in.	0·025 in.	0·020 in.	0·020 in.

GARAGING AND MAINTENANCE

When this is completed a final check should be given to see that the timing is correct.

Re-timing the Ignition. The correct ignition timings are given on page 68 and instructions for retiming are on page 103.

CARE OF TYRES

Comfort while riding, freedom from skidding, good steering, absence of hold-ups on the road, and economical running are all to a large extent dependent upon the care the rider bestows on his tyres. Whatever make of tyre is fitted on your Rudge, a large

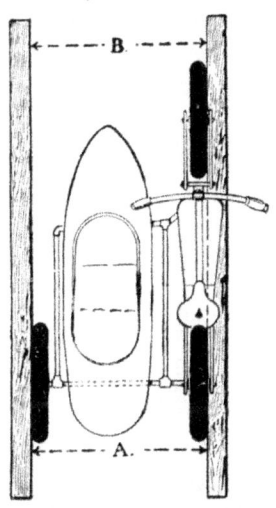

FIG. 29. CHECKING WHEEL ALIGNMENT AND SIDECAR TOE-IN BY MEANS OF BOARDS PLACED ALONG THE EDGES OF THE TYRES

mileage can be obtained with immunity from trouble if two conditions are observed. Firstly, the wheels must be kept properly aligned, and secondly the tyres must be kept correctly inflated. If either of these conditions are disregarded the tyres suffer considerably and the annual bill is higher than it should be.

Wheel Alignment. A great thief of tyre life is misalignment of wheels, and the rider would be well advised to check this alignment from time to time. This can easily be done on a solo machine with the aid of a straight piece of wood and on a sidecar machine with two similar pieces of wood.

It is, of course, absolutely essential that the edge of the board should be dead straight and square, and that it should be at least as long as the machine itself. Let us take the case of the solo motor-cycle first. Put the machine on the stand and place the straight edge of the board alongside the two tyres, as high up as possible. Then turn the front wheel until the board touches both sides of the front tyre and at least one side of the rear tyre. If the wheels are in line the board should also touch both sides of the rear wheel tyre; if it does not do so the alignment of the rear wheel must be altered by means of the chain adjusters. If correct alignment cannot be obtained it is probable that the frame or forks are twisted. On all present Rudges chain adjusters of the draw-bolt type are used only on the 250 c.c. models and on the 500 c.c. models the alignment of the wheels cannot be upset because the adjusters are of the cam type (see page 94).

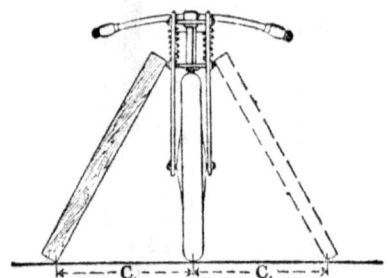

Fig. 30. If a Sidecar Machine is Vertical the Distances "C," shown Above, should be Equal

Alignment of a Sidecar Machine. When lining up a sidecar outfit the two wheels of the machine itself must first be checked in the manner described above. The board must then be set along the offside of the tyres and a similar board placed across the sidecar tyre as shown in Fig. 29. The distances between the boards at *A* and *B* must then be measured. In theory these distances should be equal, but, in practice, it is found that better steering is obtained if *B* is about ⅜ in. less than *A*. Wheel alignment is obtained by means of the sliding joint provided on the front sidecar connecting tube.

It is next necessary to make sure whether the machine itself is vertical. For this purpose the outfit must be wheeled on to a level surface and measurements must be taken from the front forks as shown in Fig. 30. In the sketch a piece of board is shown, but a walking stick or anything similar may well be used. The stick, or whatever is employed, should be rested against a given point on the front fork, and the distance between its lower extremity and the centre of the front tyre should then be measured. This distance is shown as *C* in Fig. 30.

GARAGING AND MAINTENANCE

A similar operation should then be carried out on the other side of the machine, and the two distances C should be equal. If it is found that the right-hand distance C is greater than the left-hand, it proves that the machine is leaning towards the sidecar, and adjustments to the chassis must therefore be carried out in order that a true vertical setting may be obtained. It is generally found that lighter steering is obtained by adjusting the sidecar connections so that the motor-cycle leans outwards very slightly, but on no account should it lean inwards. Vertical alignment of the motor-cycle is obtained by means of the sliding joint on the tube connecting the sidecar axle to the saddle lug. When

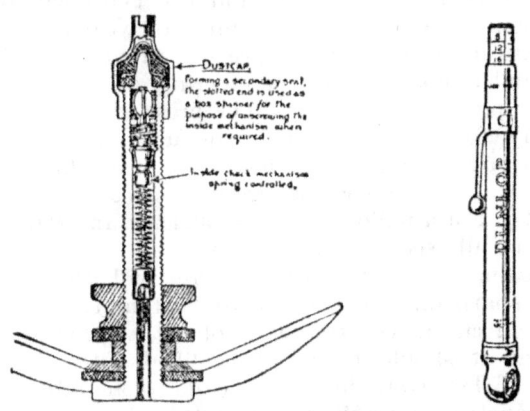

FIGS. 31, 32. SHOWING (Left) DUNLOP VALVE AND (Right) CONVENIENT PRESSURE GAUGE

the required adjustment has been made, the sidecar connections must be screwed up dead tight. Whether or not any alteration to the alignment is made it is advisable to check the sidecar connections from time to time.

The Matter of Tyre Pressure. As regards the tyres themselves, it is of primary importance that they should be inflated to the correct pressure. With the old type of tyre valve it was impossible to measure the pressure accurately, although expert riders could gauge it very nearly by appearance and feel.

All the tyres, however, are now fitted with metallic car-type valves and, with the aid of a pressure gauge, measurements can be taken accurately. Among suitable pressure gauges for all makes of tyres are: the Dunlop pencil type No. 6 gauge, the Holdtite, the Schrader No. 7750, and the Romac pressure gauge. To use a gauge, the valve dust cap (Fig. 31) is taken off, and the end of the pressure gauge is pressed on to the open end of the valve. It depresses the pin and allows air to enter the gauge and push up the piston calibrated in pounds per square inch. It is always wise to keep the dust caps screwed on, though some riders throw them away! Dust or grit getting into the valve stem is liable to interfere with the valve action of the little spring-controlled plunger (Fig. 31) and cause leakage. About once a year valve "insides" should be replaced. They can be removed by taking off the valve cap and using the slotted end as a screwdriver.

A chart of the correct inflation pressures recommended for Dunlop "Universal" tyres fitted to Rudges is given on page 54.

It must be borne in mind that under-inflation causes severe strain to be set up in the casing of the tyre. If run at too low a pressure the casings will crack and the tyres will be rendered useless when there are still many miles of wear left in the tread. Further, an unduly soft front tyre will prevent the forks acting properly and tends to upset the steering, as well as to cause the machine to pitch unpleasantly. The pressures recommended are, incidentally, for machines which are fully equipped, and if the driver and passenger are very heavy, or if a pillion passenger is habitually carried, higher pressure in the rear tyre, at any rate, is advisable. For a pillion passenger at least an extra 5 lb. per sq. in. should be allowed for the rear tyre.

It is, again, inevitable that the tyres will become cut by the glass and sharp flints which are to be found on all our roads. A superficial cut in the rubber is of little account, but it may spread, and it should therefore be filled with a suitable tyre stopping. If, however, this cut extends to the fabric of the tyre, wet will penetrate into the latter and, in due course, will rot it. Any cut of this nature should therefore be repaired efficiently. The only way to get this done is to remove the tyre and have it vulcanized.

RECOMMENDED INFLATION PRESSURES (AVON SUPREME)
(*In lb. per sq. in.* See also page 54.)

1935 Rudge Model	Front Solo	Front Sidecar	Rear Solo	Rear Sidecar	Sidecar Wheel
250 c.c. Tourist (25 × 3)	18	—	22	—	—
250 c.c. Sports (26 × 3)	18	—	22	—	—
500 c.c. Special (26 × 3·25)	18	18	20	28	16
500 c.c. "Ulster" (27 × 3, F. 27 × 3·25, R)	23	24	19	28	16

Obviously, if long tyre life is sought, freak hills and extremely rough surfaces should be avoided. Wheel spin in particular is

GARAGING AND MAINTENANCE

extremely detrimental to the rear tyre. The majority of riders never subject their tyres to these exceptional conditions, but many of them do not appreciate the strain which they impose on their tyres by bad driving. Fierce braking, rapid acceleration and fast cornering (particularly on a sidecar machine) should be avoided as far as possible, the same applying to quick engagement of the clutch with a wide throttle opening. This latter procedure, incidentally, is also detrimental to the transmission system. Two important points not yet mentioned are: (a) avoid crossing upraised tram lines or rubbing on the kerb; (b) do not allow the tyres to stand in patches of oil or paraffin.

Smooth Tyres are Illegal. There is one point which solo riders in particular should remember. When a tyre tread becomes worn right off a new tyre must be fitted as it is now illegal to run with smooth tyres. A badly worn tread should be treated with great care. A solo machine should never be driven at high speeds when either of its tyres is in this condition. The tyres fitted to all Rudges are of the wired-on type, and upon rapid deflation they do not leave the rim as was possible with the old pattern beaded-edge tyres. If a machine is driven at high speeds, however, and the front tyre suddenly bursts a crash is almost inevitable.

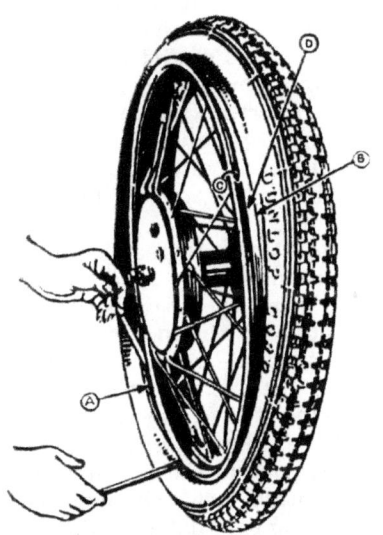

FIG. 33. HOW TO REMOVE A FRONT COVER

The tyre edges at A cannot be levered off until the edges at B are first pushed down into the well-base rim D off the rim C

For tyres to give best results they should be checked for pressure every week or fortnight, and if found to be below the recommended pressure should be inflated accordingly. At the same time they should be examined carefully throughout their circumference; any tiny flints found embedded in the rubber should be removed, and any cuts should be repaired to prevent the ingress of water.

Tyre Removal. A few words on the subject of removing and refitting tyres may not be out of place, and those new to motorcycling would do well to acquaint themselves with the correct procedure, so that when the unexpected puncture does occur a minimum amount of time and patience is required to effect a repair. It is by no means an uncommon sight to witness a motor-cyclist *struggling* to remove a tyre, and through faulty refitting the tube is sometimes pinched and a second repair becomes necessary. Tyre removal and replacement need offer no difficulty whatever if a few simple precautions are taken. All Rudge motor-cycles are now fitted with heavy duty tyres which have inextensible wired edges fitting into well-base rims. To remove this type of tyre, first completely deflate it by removing all the valve parts, including the check mechanism (Fig. 31). Then, at a point opposite the valve, push the edges of the cover into the well-base rim. Proceed to remove the tyre edge as shown in Fig. 33, by inserting two small levers, one each side of the valve about 4 in. apart. No force should be necessary *as long as the edges of the tyre opposite the valve are right down in the rim*. Gradually work round until the whole of the tyre edge comes off the rim, enabling the tube to be withdrawn. Do not employ large tyre levers.

Refitting a Tyre. Assuming one edge of the tyre is already in position, slightly inflate the inner tube, insert it inside the cover, and push the valve stem through the hole in the rim. Do not tighten up the lock-nut securing the valve to the rim, and also see that the tube is not twisted. Then start to fit the second edge of the cover at a point diametrically opposite the valve, by placing it over the rim and pushing it down into the rim base. Push on the rest of the cover and, with a pair of small tyre levers, work round each side in such a way that the part near the valve is refitted last. On no account use excessive force, and while inflating see that the edges of the cover bed down evenly on the rim. A mark moulded on the rubber should be at an even distance from the rim all round. Finally, replace the valve lock-nut and pump up the tyre to the recommended pressure. After a puncture has been repaired do not immediately pump up to full pressure, but give the patch a chance to stick on hard. In connection with punctures, the following two points are important: (a) See that the solution is "tacky" before applying the patch, (b) don't be stingy with the french chalk.

CARBURETTOR-TUNING AND MAINTENANCE

The working of the semi-automatic needle jet Amal carburettor has already been described on page 42, and Fig. 19 shows a sectional view of the carburettor. New machines are sent out with the carburettor carefully tuned to give the best all-round performance. It is not wise to alter the original setting or jet sizes (see table on page 76) without good reason, but this may be necessary to meet special climatic conditions or to get the best results for speed work.

GARAGING AND MAINTENANCE

Tuning the Amal Carburettor. Should the setting of this instrument not give entire satisfaction for particular requirements, there are four separate ways of rectifying matters as given herewith, and the adjustment should be made in this order: (a) Main jet (three-quarters to full throttle); (b) pilot air adjustment (closed to one-eighth throttle); (c) throttle valve cut-away on the air-intake side (one-eighth to one-quarter throttle); (d) needle position (one-quarter to three-quarters throttle). The diagram (Fig. 34) clearly indicates the part of the throttle range over which each adjustment is effective.

(a) To obtain the correct main jet size, several jets should be experimented with, and that selected should be the *smallest which gives maximum power and speed on full throttle.*

(b) To weaken slow-running mixture, screw pilot air adjuster outwards, and to enrich screw pilot air adjuster inwards.

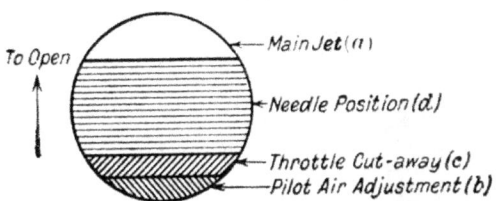

FIG. 34. RANGE AND SEQUENCE OF ADJUSTMENTS—
AMAL CARBURETTOR

Screw pilot air adjuster home in a clockwise direction. Place gear lever in "neutral." Slightly flood the float chamber by gently depressing the tickler until fuel begins to escape from the mixing chamber. Set magneto at half advance, throttle approximately one-eighth open, close the air lever, start the engine, and warm up. After warming up, reduce the engine revolutions by gently throttling down. The slow-running mixture will prove over-rich unless air leaks exist. Very gradually unscrew the pilot jet adjuster. The engine speed will increase, and must again be reduced by gently closing the throttle until, by a combination of throttle position and air adjustment, the desired "idling" is obtained. It is occasionally necessary to retard completely the magneto before getting a satisfactory tick-over, especially when early ignition timing is used. If it is desired to make the engine idle with the throttle quite closed, the position of the throttle valve must be set by means of the throttle stop-screw, the throttle lever during this adjustment being pushed right home. Alternatively, if the screw is adjusted clear of the throttle valve, the engine will be shut off in the normal way by the control lever.

(c) Given satisfactory "tick-over," set the magneto control at half-advance with the air lever fully open. Very slowly open the throttle valve when, if the engine responds regularly up to one-quarter throttle, the valve cut-away is correct.

A weak mixture is indicated by spitting back through the air-intake with blue flames and hesitation in picking up, which disappears when the air lever is closed down. This can be remedied by fitting a throttle valve with less cut-away. A rich mixture is shown by a black, sooty exhaust, and the engine falters when the air valve is closed. The remedy for this is a throttle valve with greater cut-away. Each Amal valve is stamped with two numbers, the first indicating the type number of the carburettor, and the second figure the amount of cut-away on the intake side of the valve in sixteenths of an inch, e.g. 6/4 is a type 6 valve with four-sixteenths in. or a ¼ in. cut-away.

AMAL CARBURETTOR SETTINGS FOR 1935-9 RUDGES

Model	Main Jet	Throttle Valve	Needle Position	Needle Jet
250 c.c. Sports	130	6/4	3	·1065
250 c.c. Tourist, Rapid	120	5/4	3	·1065
500 c.c. Special	150	6/4	2	·1065
500 c.c. "Ulster"	150	29/5	3	·109

(d) Open air lever fully and the throttle half-way. Note if the exhaust is crisp and the engine flexible. Close the air valve slightly below the throttle, when the exhaust note and engine revolutions should remain constant. Should popping back and spitting occur with blue flames from the intake, the mixture is weak, and the needle should be slightly raised. Test by lowering the air valve gently. The engine revolutions will rise when the air valve is lowered slightly below the throttle valve.

If the engine speed does not increase progressively with raising of the throttle, and a smoky exhaust is apparent with heavy laboured running, and tendency to eight-stroke, the mixture is too rich and the needle should be lowered in the throttle valve. Having found the correct needle position, the carburettor setting is now complete, and it will be found that the driving is practically automatic once the engine is warmed up. For speed work the main jet may be increased by 10 per cent, when the air lever should be fully open on full throttle.

Cleaning the Amal Carburettor. Periodical cleaning is necessary to maintain efficient functioning of the carburettor, and should be carried out in the following sequence.

GARAGING AND MAINTENANCE

Disconnect petrol pipe. Unscrew the jet plug Q (Fig. 19) and remove float chamber complete. With box or set spanner, slacken the mixing chamber union nut E. Mixing chamber complete may now be removed from engine, either by unscrewing the clip pin (if outlet) or the bolts (if flange fitting). Unscrew mixing chamber lock ring, and pull out throttle valve needle and air valve. Remove main jet P and needle jet O. Mixing chamber union nut E may then be removed and jet block complete pushed out. If this is obstinate, tap gently, using a wooden stump inside the mixing chamber. Unscrew float chamber cover W and slacken lock screw X. Withdraw the float by pinching the clip V inwards, and at the same time pull gently upwards.

Generally it is sufficient to wash all the parts in clean petrol, but if the carburettor has had extended service, check the following—

(a) FLOAT CHAMBER NEEDLE U. If a distinct shoulder is visible on the point of seating, renew this as soon as convenient.

(b) THROTTLE VALVE. Test in mixing chamber, and if excessive play is present it is advisable to renew this without delay.

(c) THROTTLE NEEDLE CLIP. This part must securely grip needle. *Free rotation must not take place*, otherwise the needle groove will become worn and necessitate a new part being fitted. *Be sure to refit the clip in the same groove.*

(d) JET BLOCK. If trouble has been experienced with erratic "idling," ascertain by means of a fine bristle that the pilot jet J is clear, and that the pilot outlet M in the mixing chamber is unobstructed.

To Reassemble. Refit jet block F with washer on underside, and screw on lightly mixing chamber union nut E. Screw in needle jet O and main jet P. Open air lever $\frac{7}{8}$ in., throttle lever half-way; grasp the air slide between the thumb and the finger; *make sure that the needle enters the central hole in the adapter top.* Slightly turn the throttle valve until it enters the adapter guide, when on pushing down the valves the air valve should enter its guide. If not, slightly move the mixing chamber top, when the air valve will slide into place. Screw on mixing chamber lock-nut. *No brute force is necessary.*

Attach carburettor to the cylinder, pushing right home, and examine washer if flange fitting. Insert the jet plug Q, and thoroughly tighten union nut E by means of a fixed spanner. Refit float and needle, holding the needle head against its seating by means of a pencil until the float and the clip V are slipped into position. Make sure that the clip enters the groove provided. Screw on the cover tightly and lock in position by means of the lock screw X. Fit holding bolt in float chamber with one washer above and one below the lug. Screw the jet plug into union nut E

and lock securely. Clean petrol pipe and filter if fitted, and replace. It will be necessary to re-check the pilot setting if this has been disturbed.

MAINTENANCE OF IGNITION AND LIGHTING SYSTEMS

On the 500 c.c. Rudges separate dynamos and magnetos are used, but on the 250 c.c. models combined generators are used. It is therefore proposed to deal with both the ignition and lighting systems in this section. As the ignition system is of greater importance we will consider this first.

Always Run on a Suitable Plug. Engines are fastidious in regard to sparking plugs and it is essential always to fit a plug of the correct type.

A suitable 14 mm. Lodge plug for the 1939 Ulster models is the HLN. On other Rudges, where an 18 mm. plug is needed, fit a Lodge H1 or H1P. Use an H14 (14 mm.) plug elsewhere. A suitable K.L.G. plug for the 1933-9 Special, T.T. Replica models, and the 499 c.c. Silver Vase Special, is the M80 (18 mm.). On the 250 c.c. Rapid and 1934-8 Ulster, fit an F70 (14 mm.). For the 1939 Ulster, use an FE70 (14 mm.). On other machines use the M60 (18 mm.).

Keep Plug Clean and Points Adjusted. Difficult starting or occasional misfiring can usually be traced to a dirty or defective sparking plug.

The life of a plug is considerable, but the points of the electrodes gradually burn away and eventually the gap becomes enlarged considerably, and it is necessary to reset the points with the aid of a feeler gauge. The correct gap is 0·018 in.–0·020 in. A gap of 0·018 gives excellent slow-running, but on 250 c.c. Sports and 500 c.c. "Ulster" models which have high compression engines it is best to use a gap of about 0·015 at the plug. Excessive gap at the plug points means that the voltage required from the magneto is higher; and this not only renders starting difficult, but—what is worse—causes brush discharge inside the magneto. This discharge eventually causes internal corrosion, and the efficiency of the magneto is impaired. From time to time the plug should be removed and thoroughly cleaned with petrol, both inside and outside. All deposits of soot or charred oil must be eliminated, as these are apt to cause leakage and bad running. The insulation should be examined for cracks or flaws, and in very humid weather should be wiped dry with a rag before starting-up. The accepted method of testing for current at the plug terminal is to place a wooden-handled screw-driver, with steel blade, across the terminal and just touching the cylinder fin, when a spark

GARAGING AND MAINTENANCE

should be visible on rotating the engine. To test the plug itself, remove it with the H.T. lead still affixed, clean it, lay it on the cylinder, and note whether it sparks satisfactorily when the engine is rotated.

It is advisable occasionally to dismantle the sparking plug in order to clean the inside thoroughly. This is most easily accomplished by holding the body nut (large hexagon) in a vice and unscrewing the gland nut (small hexagon). Be careful not to scrape the insulation on the centre electrode, or this may flake off and cause pre-ignition. Clean the carbon from inside the body with an old pen-knife, and on reassembly do not overlook the copper washer.

The Contact-breaker. The magneto should not be interfered with unnecessarily, for it is a very delicate instrument and functions best when left well alone; but at regular intervals, say every 1,000 miles, the contact-breaker cover should be removed and the contacts (see Fig. 35) should be examined, and their gap checked with a 12 thou' feeler gauge. If the clearance is excessive, the timing will be advanced and the primary circuit will not be closed for the correct period, and occasional misfiring is very likely. Provided the contacts are kept clean and, above all, *free from oil,* they will probably need adjustment only at long intervals. It is not desirable to alter the setting unless the gap varies considerably from that of the magneto spanner gauge.

Lucas M.L. To clean the points, remove the screw securing the small spring blade which carries the moving point. This blade may be removed, leaving both points accessible for cleaning. When replacing, see that the small backing spring is placed with its convex side next to the spring blade. If this is replaced with its concave side towards the blade, breakage will probably occur. While the spring blade is removed, take off the contact-breaker and inspect the push-rod. If this shows any signs of sticking, it should be carefully cleaned and oiled.

To remove the control cable from the case, undo the hexagon nut and draw the cable upwards to its utmost extent, when it may be found that the nipple may be slipped sideways out of the hole in the plunger, and this may be assisted by levering upwards on the end of the plunger visible inside the contact-breaker cover.

B.T.-H. Magneto. The contact-breaker points of this instrument can easily be cleaned without the necessity of removing the contact-breaker lever. Although if this is more convenient it can easily be done by swinging round the lever spring and gently prising off the lever from its pivot. Adjustment of the gap is carried out by screwing in or out the contact mounted in the centre block of the contact-breaker, and should always be carefully locked with a locknut provided, after making an adjustment.

On the B.T.-H. magneto the contacts are made slightly convex and if the points are dirty they should be cleaned with *very fine* emery cloth. Under no circumstances file the points, which must be kept absolutely clean and free from oil. See that the rubber sleeve is a tight fit over the Bowden advance and retard cable casing and if perished renew it. Remove the collector mouldings and wipe the taper portions with a clean dry cloth. See that the carbon brushes are free in their holders. Insert a twisted-up corner of the cloth in the aperture exposed on removing the collector moulding, and revolve the armature once or twice. This will get rid of any carbon dust on the slip-ring flanges.

Locating Troubles. If ignition trouble is suspected, remove the high tension lead and see if a spark occurs when the high tension terminal is held near the cylinder when the engine is rotated. If so, try another plug. If not, remove the contact-breaker cover and see that the points are dry, clean, correctly adjusted, and working properly. Examine the high tension lead for cracks or breakage, and see that the insulation has not been burnt against the cylinder fins. If all seems in order, take out the bakelite high tension terminal, rotate the magneto, and see whether any shock can be felt by touching the slip-ring with the end of a lead pencil, and see that the carbon brush is free to slide. If no fault can be found and the interior of the magneto appears dry, return it to the makers. Do not remove the armature from the magneto, since by doing so you will demagnetize it, and, owing to its construction, it cannot be remagnetized except by a special machine.

To Remove Cable Control. It is necessary to remove the plug at the bottom of the contact-breaker housing, when the cable itself will protrude. The split washer fitting over the cable nipple, together with its casing, can then be detached by unscrewing the adjusting screw and locknut situated on the upper end of the housing.

The "Maglita." Generally speaking, the remarks relating to the magneto also apply to the ignition part of the Maglita, thus the gap between the contact-breaker points should be 0·012 in., the thickness of the gauge on the magneto spanner, and a spot of oil should be placed on the cam about every 1,000 miles. The complete contact-breaker may be taken away for inspection by removing the two vertical screws at the side of the contact-breaker **blade.** When lubricating the face cam remember the oil hole under the contact-breaker and do not forget the lubricator on the spindle end.

As regards the lighting part of the unit, see that the commutator

GARAGING AND MAINTENANCE

is clean, that the brushes are free in their guides and not unduly worn, and that all connections are sound. Do not attempt to interfere with the centrifugal cut-out, for you can definitely test whether it is faulty without removing it.

Supposing that the ammeter does not read when the engine is running and the switch on "Charge," this indicates that the generator is not charging. Take a short piece of wire and, with the engine running and with the lamps switched on, connect the positive terminal to that of the collector brush, and finally to the brush itself. If the lamps light, the trouble is with the

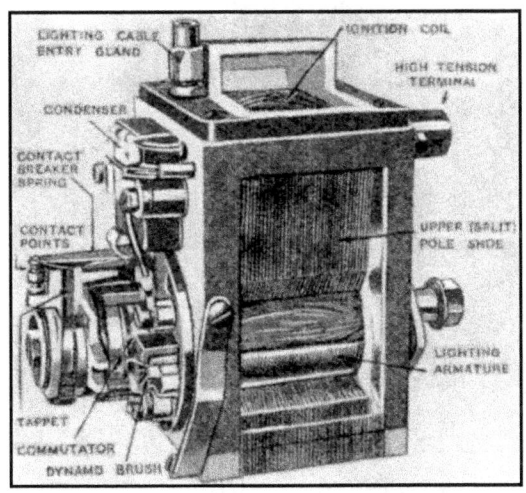

Fig. 35. Lucas "Maglita" with Covers Removed to Show Details

cut-out, and if there is still no improvement it may be that the cable from the generator to the head lamp switch is broken or shorting, so disconnect the wire from the positive terminal and connect this to the top of the generator through a spare lamp. If this should light, it indicates that the fault lies in the outside wiring. Here again, do not attempt to remove the armature since the instrument will become demagnetized.

"Maglita" Wiring. A wiring diagram for the "Maglita" ignition and lighting systems will be found on page 82. If there is occasion to alter the wiring, first disconnect the battery to avoid the possibility of short-circuiting it. The lead from the positive battery terminal is connected to the B terminal of the centre-zero ammeter on the headlamp, and the connection must be done up tightly. Be careful not to connect up the battery in the reverse

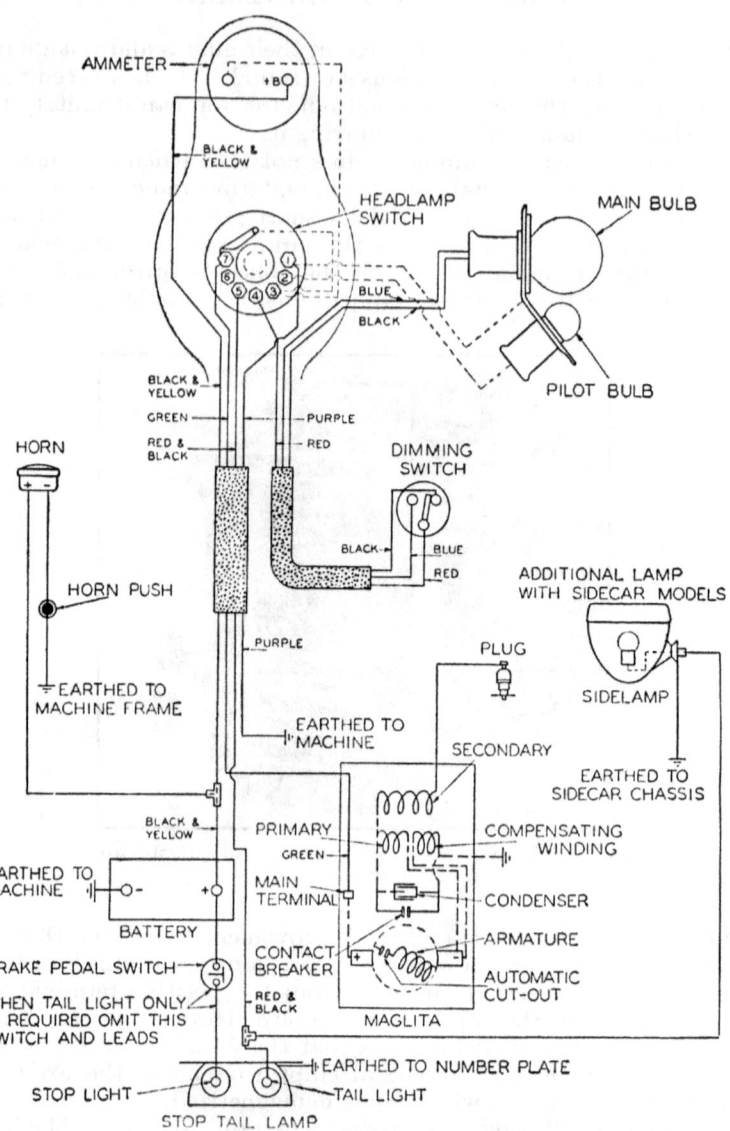

FIG 36. WIRING DIAGRAM FOR LUCAS "MAGLITA" LIGHTING AND IGNITION EQUIPMENT (WITH DU42M HEADLAMP) FITTED ON 250 c.c. RUDGES

All internal connections are shown dotted and the cable ends are identified by means of coloured sleevings, as indicated on the diagram. The stop light connections do not apply to the Tourist Model

GARAGING AND MAINTENANCE 83

direction as this may partially demagnetize the magnets of the "Maglita." Wiring should be always carried out with 5 mm. rubber-covered ignition cable.

The Miller Dynamo. As a general rule, the DM3T Miller dynamo gives long and satisfactory service, with practically no attention. There are, however, a few rather important points that should be observed.

Warning. *Before making any adjustments to the headlamp or dynamo, disconnect one or both of the battery terminal connections.* Failure to do this may incur a burnt-out ammeter or a reversal of the dynamo polarity.

Commutator and Brushes. When in position, each brush should press firmly on the commutator. Periodically the commutator and brushes should be inspected, and all traces of carbon dust and grease should be removed. To clean a blackened or dirty commutator, use fine glass paper. If the commutator has a highly-polished surface (dark bronze colour), leave well alone.

It is advisable to change the brushes before they are worn out, as this will prevent the sparking which gives rise to blackening of the commutator and unsteady charging current, owing to the brushes making imperfect contact. Use only brushes of Miller manufacture, as these are specially made for the dynamo.

Cut-out. Except for an occasional inspection of the contacts to ensure that these are clean, the cut-out calls for no attention whatever; it is, in fact, best left untouched except by experts.

Reversed Dynamo Polarity. Should the polarity of the dynamo be accidentally reversed due to touching together or shorting with a spanner the + D. and S.H. dynamo terminals, it is necessary to reverse the battery connections temporarily, and again make contact between the + D. and S.H. terminals, in order to restore the dynamo to normal and obtain a charge. After making contact between the + D. and S.H. terminals, the battery connections should be changed back again, when on starting up the engine with the switch on "charge" the dynamo will function correctly.

Lubrication. This matter is dealt with on page 48. Avoid using too much grease when lubricating the commutator side bearing, or it may reach the commutator and cause trouble.

Miller Wiring. A wiring diagram for the Miller lighting system on the 500 c.c. Rudges will be found on page 84. If any alterations are made to the wiring, first see that the battery is disconnected* and use only Miller cable terminal ends. All connections must be kept clean and tight. When fitting a high frequency electric horn, it should be noted that the lead supplying

* Failure to do this may burn out the ammeter or reverse the dynamo polarity.

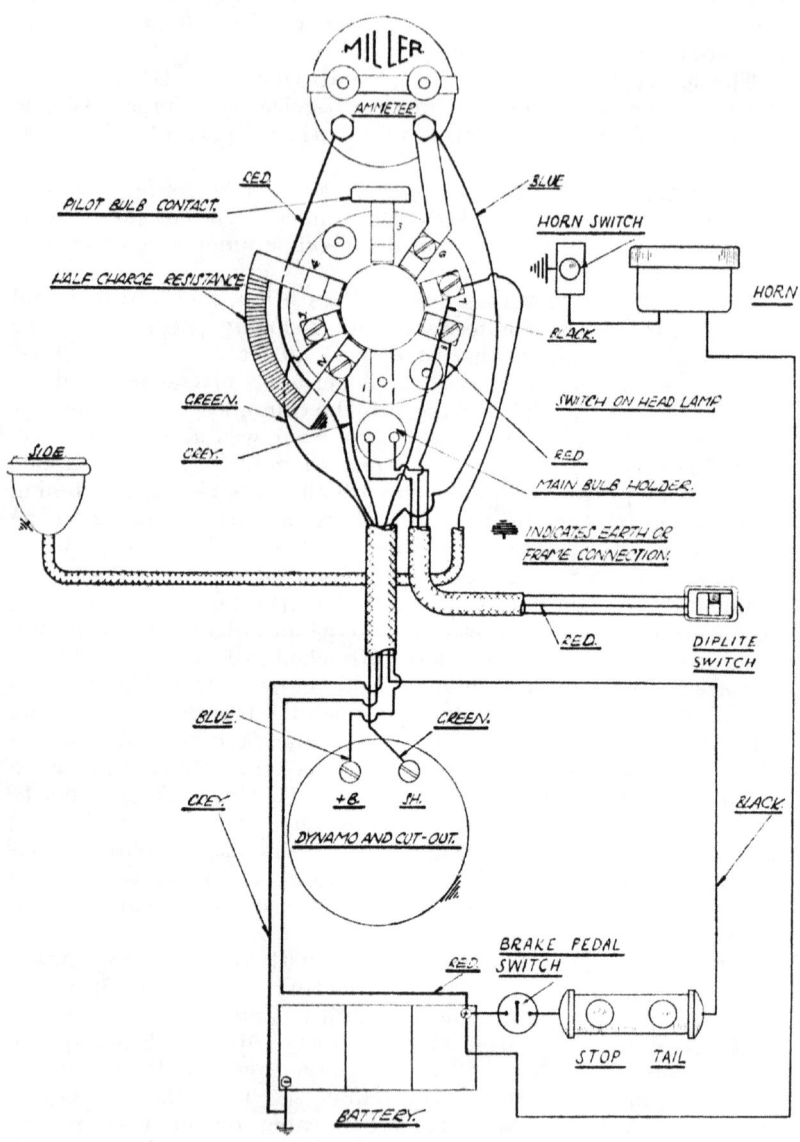

Fig. 37. Wiring Diagram for Miller Dynamo Lighting Equipment (with 74E Headlamp) Fitted on the 500 c.c. Rudges

GARAGING AND MAINTENANCE 85

current to the horn should be taken direct from the battery positive terminal. The earthing wire is taken from the horn to the push-switch fitted on the right-hand side of the handlebars.

Do Not Run with Dynamo Chain too Tight. This is important because if the chain is excessively tight the armature bearings may be overloaded and possibly the conductors may become fractured.

Look After the Battery. It is of the utmost importance that the battery should receive regular attention to keep it in good condition.

The following are the most important maintenance hints—

1. Keep the acid level to just above the top of the plates.
2. Add only distilled water, never tap water.
3. Test the specific gravity of the acid with a hydrometer occasionally.
4. The battery must never be left in a discharged condition.

Topping-up. At least once a month the vent plugs in the top of the battery should be removed and the level of the acid solution examined. If necessary, distilled water, which can be obtained at all chemists and most garages, should be added to bring the level just above the tops of the plates. For convenience, top-up with a battery filler. If, however, acid solution has been spilled, it should be replaced by a diluted sulphuric acid solution of correct specific gravity, obtainable from an electrician. In order to top-up it is not necessary to remove the battery. You only need to remove the central screw which secures the battery cover, when the vent plugs are exposed to view. It is important when examining the cells that naked lights should not be held near the vents, on account of the possible danger of igniting the gas coming from the plates.

Storage. If the equipment is laid by for several months, the battery must be given a small charge from a separate source of electrical energy about once a fortnight, in order to obviate any permanent sulphation of the plates. In no circumstances must the electrolyte be removed from the battery and the plates allowed to dry, as certain chemical changes take place which result in permanent loss of capacity. This change is known as sulphation.

Testing the Condition of the Battery. It is advisable to check occasionally the specific gravity of the acid, as this gives a very good indication of the state of charge of the battery.

An instrument known as a "hydrometer" is employed for this purpose. These can be bought at any Lucas or Miller Service Depot. Voltmeter readings of each cell do not provide a reliable indication of the condition of the battery, unless special precautions are taken.

How to Use the Hydrometer. First see that the acid is at the correct level and that the electrolyte is thoroughly mixed. To ensure the latter condition, hydrometer readings should be taken after a run on the motor-cycle. To use the Lucas hydrometer, the instrument should be held vertically over the battery cell and after compressing the bulb the red rubber tube should be dipped as far as possible into the electrolyte. Then gradually release the bulb until the acid solution rises in the body and lifts the hydrometer float about one inch. Now remove the hydrometer and note the scale reading at the surface of the electrolyte. This reading shows the density or specific gravity. When taking the reading avoid letting the float touch the bulb.

After taking the S.G. return the solution to the cell, and take the S.G. of the other cells. If one cell reading differs greatly from the remainder possibly some of the acid has escaped or there may be a short between the plates. In such a case expert attention is required. The correct S.G. readings for the Lucas 12 amp. hr. battery are as follows: fully charged, 1·285–1·300; about half discharged, about 1·210; fully discharged, about 1·150. In the case of the Exide 13 amp. hr. battery used with the Miller dynamo the specific gravity readings are about the same. Charge up immediately if the S.G. falls as low as 1·150.

Battery-charging Period. It is difficult to lay down rigid instructions on this subject, as the conditions under which motor-cycles are used vary considerably; and, obviously, the amount of charging a battery will require is directly dependent on the extent to which the lamps are used. The following suggestions will serve as a rough guide.

On a solo machine used normally, and not left standing for long periods at night with the lights on, daylight charging with the switch in the *C* position should be not less than about 50 per cent of the night running with the switch in the *H* position. With a sidecar outfit the period of daylight charging may be equal to the night running, and when an electric horn is fitted generous daylight charging is recommended. As a rule, little or no harm follows overcharging so long as gassing and waste of acid is not caused, but undercharging is definitely harmful and eventually causes sulphated and permanently damaged plates. This time should only be increased if the period of night running is considerable, or when the battery is found to be in a low state of charge (if the specific gravity of the acid solution is 1·210 or below). The chief ill-effect of overcharging is loss of acid by gassing. Overcharging calls for frequent topping up also.

The battery must never be left in a fully-discharged condition, and unless some long runs are to be taken, it is advisable to have the battery removed from the machine and charged up from an independent electrical supply.

Cleaning Reflectors. The reflectors are protected by a transparent and colourless covering, which enables any accidental finger marks to be removed with a soft cloth or chamois leather without affecting the surface of the reflectors. On no account should a metal polish be used on lamp reflectors, as this is liable to ruin the surfaces. If the ebony black of the outer body becomes dull in service, the original lustre can be restored by the application of a little good furniture or car polish.

Focusing Headlamp. The best method of focusing is to take the motor-cycle to a straight, level road, find the correct bulb adjustment, and then move the lamp in its adjustable mounting until the best road position is obtained. The driving light should be switched on when focusing is carried out. Special care should be taken to see that the filament is in its correct position relative to the reflector.

In the case of the Lucas headlamp it is necessary to detach the reflector and then loosen the clip which clamps the bulb holder. The holder can then be moved backwards or forwards until the correct focus is obtained. With the Miller headlamp insert the bulb in the usual manner, but when the bayonet pins have arrived home apply a further twisting force to the right which will enable both the bulb holder and bulb to slide backwards or forwards until correct focus is obtained. As soon as the extra twisting force is removed the bulb is securely held.

Replacement of Bulbs. Always use genuine Miller or Lucas bulbs and reflectors. It is safe to use 3 amp. main bulbs for the headlamps and 5 amp. bulbs for the pilot, tail, and sidecar lamps. For the Miller headlamp use 6 volt, 18 watt bulbs, and for the Lucas headlamp 6 volt, 12 watt bulbs, both of the diplite double-contact type. For the pilot, tail, and sidecar lamps use 6 volt, 3 watt, single-centre contact bulbs. Gas-filled bulbs besides giving a brighter light are more economical to use than the vacuum type.

If the Stop Light Fails. Suspect incorrect adjustment of the switch relative to the brake-operating mechanism. On the 250 c.c. Sports model (the Tourist Model has no stop light) adjust by moving along the operating key attached to the brake rod. On the 500 c.c. models slacken the hexagon nut and swivel the switch box.

VARIOUS ADJUSTMENTS (1933-6)

Valve Clearances. One of the possible sources of lack of power is incorrect adjustment of the valve clearances. As all Rudge machines have overhead valves it is important to check the clearances when the engine is *cold*, since when the engine is hot these clearances increase somewhat, and should the adjustment be taken up when the engine is hot there would be no compression after it had cooled.

With the 500 c.c. "Special" machine the only point where adjustment is required is on the tappets. The inlet push-rod should be just free to rotate without appreciable up and down movement, but in the case of the exhaust a clearance of 0·004 in. between the rocker and the valve stem should be given.

With the radial valve engines there is individual adjustment between each valve. The right-hand inlet and exhaust valves are first adjusted by means of the tappet rods, just as in the case of the "Special" machines, but after this has been done the clearance on the other valves should be checked and, if necessary, adjusted independently. On radial valve engines and exhaust side of the "Ulster" machines this is effected by adjusting up the nuts on the pillar which supports the side plates which carry the rocker spindles. This adjustment does not affect the righthand valve, but it should always be done after the latter has been correctly adjusted. The clearance given should be the same as on the "Special" machine; that is, 0·004 in. on the exhaust valves and practically nothing on the inlet valves.

As a precaution, the engine should be rotated until it is on the compression stroke when the clearances are being checked. A very large clearance would cause the engine to be noisy, to overheat, and to hammer the valve seats very severely.

To adjust the tappets it is first necessary to uncover them by removing the bottom half of the telescopic tube, and to do this loosen the nut at the base of the tube, rotate the bottom half of the tube until it is released, then push it up. Now hold the tappet head (*A*, Fig. 38) with one spanner and with another spanner slacken the locknut (*B*). Then hold the hexagon (*C*) with the small end of the thin hook spanner and screw the tappet head either up or down until you have obtained the correct clearance between the rocker and the valve. Afterwards re-tighten the locknut (*B*).

It will be more convenient to adjust the exhaust tappet if the inlet push-rod is removed, and to do this on the 500 c.c. "Special" machine remove the rocker cover plate, rotate the engine until the inlet valve is lifted, insert the closed ended spanner below the tappet rocker with the front end of the spanner raised on the ledge at the back of the cover, and turn the engine until the tappet drops, when the push-rod may be withdrawn. If it is desired to remove the exhaust tappet, rotate the engine until the exhaust rocker is lifted and insert the sheet metal spanner between the exhaust lifter cam and rocker. This will hold up the rocker and enable the exhaust push-rod to be withdrawn when the engine is turned. Replace in the reverse order.

Fig. 38. Tappet Adjustment (500 c.c. "Special")

To remove the inlet push-rod from the radial valve engines, raise the inlet rocker by means of a small screwdriver levered on the front rocker support plate. The illustration (Fig. 39) shows this quite clearly. It may be more convenient to rotate the engine until the rocker is lifted and merely use the screwdriver as a means of retaining the rocker while the push-rod is removed.

On the 250 c.c. Tourist model the front overhead rocker support plate has two nuts provided to serve as a fulcrum for a small screwdriver when it is desired to remove the tappets.

Twist-grip Adjustment. The throttle control can be adjusted for tightness by means of the small grub screw which can be seen on the metal ring at the outer end of the rotating control. Quite a

FIG. 39. REMOVING TAPPET ON RADIAL VALVE ENGINE

small alteration of this screw will appreciably alter the degree of stiffness of the twist grip. Some riders like a loose action, others a stiff one.

Keep Backlash in Exhaust Valve Lifter Control. This is necessary to prevent the exhaust lifter cam touching the rocker when the engine is running. The handlebar lever should not begin to raise the exhaust valve until it has moved about one-third of its travel. Slacken the locknut at the cable stop and screw the stop in or out until this backlash is obtained.

Also Maintain Backlash in Clutch Cable. Loosen the locknut and adjust the screw bearing on the end of the clutch push-rod until slight backlash is present at the clutch lever. It is only possible

GARAGING AND MAINTENANCE

to remove the adjusting screw from the inside of the operating lever. Keep the cable and push-rod lubricated.

To Remove Gear Box Shield. To remove the shield fitted to all 1935 models except the 250 c.c. models, remove the footrest crank and unscrew the pair of knurled nuts securing the shield. When upswept exhaust pipes are fitted, the bottom edge of the shield must first be brought out clear of the brake pedal and removed after rotating the kickstarter lever to a horizontal position. If difficulty occurs, remove the exhaust pipe.

To Obtain Good Braking. Keep all exposed joints, threads and cables well lubricated. With the machine jacked up, check that both wheels freely revolve with the brake pedal hard against its

FIG. 40. SHOWING REAR BRAKE AND CHAIN ADJUSTMENT

stop. On depressing the pedal about $\frac{1}{2}$ in., both brakes should begin to operate together, or else the front one slightly before the rear. Adjust by means of the hexagon nut (F, Fig. 40) and the hexagon-headed stop and lock nut (C, Fig. 42) situated on the side of the front forks. The hand control may be adjusted by means of the hand adjustment on the front forks. This hand adjustment should be made so that the brake is applied without excessive stretching of the hand. The hand control exerts a very powerful braking effect and the control, on machines with cable-operated brakes, is fixed to the brake lever so that less leverage obtains than is the case with the cable from the brake pedal.

If Oil Gets on the Brake Shoes. Remove the wheel and brake parts and scrub the shoes with petrol. See that the cam and its shaft are well greased, but remove any grease or oil which may have exuded from the wheel hub.

To Adjust Wheel Bearings. It is unnecessary to remove the wheel. Slacken off the locknut and adjust the loose cone by means of the slots in the dust cover. Tighten the locknut and to make sure the wheel is free, spin it by hand. In the case of the 250 c.c. models adjust by turning the adjustable cone on the near side with the dust cover as on the 500 c.c. models.

To Remove Front Wheel. On the 500 c.c. machines the wheels are interchangeable and quickly detachable. To detach the 500 c.c. front wheel remove the knock-out spindle and the brake anchor pin, and disconnect the speedometer cable at the lower end. Remove the wheel and leave the anchor plate and brake shoes attached to the control cables. When replacing with another wheel take the internal sleeve from the left side of the hollow spindle (500 c.c. only) and transfer to the new wheel.

How to Detach Rear Mudguard. Access to and removal of the rear wheel from all models have been rendered extremely convenient by the fitting of a completely detachable rear mudguard. All that is necessary is to remove the short bolts attaching the front end of this mudguard to the brazed lugs on the back stay, and to slacken off the nuts which secure the mudguard stays to the back forks until the cylindrical portion of each nut is clear of the hole in the stays. On 250 c.c. Tourist machines these nuts must be completely removed from the bolt before the mudguard stays can be detached. After disconnecting the lighting wires at the detachable plugs, the whole of the mudguard can be completely taken away.

To Remove Rear Wheel. To remove the 500 c.c. rear wheel, remove the brake anchor pin, disengage the brake control by means of the quick-release device, undo the knock-out spindle nut (left side) and remove the knock-out spindle and sleeve (right side). Move the wheel to the right and disengage the sleeve from the left frame jaw. The wheel is then free to drop and may be pushed forward so that the chain may be unhooked from the sprocket.

When a spare wheel is to be fitted change the brake mechanism to the spare wheel and replace in the reverse order, noting that the keys in the left sleeve and washer engage with the slot in the spindle.

The back fork ends on the 250 c.c. frame are of the forward drop-out type. After the brake anchor pin has been removed and the brake rod uncoupled, the spindle nuts slackened off and the drawbolts pulled sideways, the wheel will drop out of the frame and the chain can then be unhooked and the wheel removed.

Primary Chain Adjustment. The primary chain runs together with the dynamo or "Maglita" chain enclosed in an oil-bath chain case, and therefore wear and stretch occur very gradually. The tension of the chain may be examined by means of the inspection cover, through which a finger may be inserted. The chain

GARAGING AND MAINTENANCE

at its tightest point should have a total up-and-down movement midway between the sprockets of $\frac{3}{8}$ in. to $\frac{1}{2}$ in. Avoid excessive tightness as well as slackness.

To adjust the primary chain on the 500 c.c. models, slacken the gearbox bolts and also the large nut (C, Fig. 41) immediately underneath the rear of the gearbox, and slide the box backwards or forwards with a box spanner applied to the small hexagon (D) which projects from the larger one just referred to. This rotates a crank connected in the gearbox body by a link.

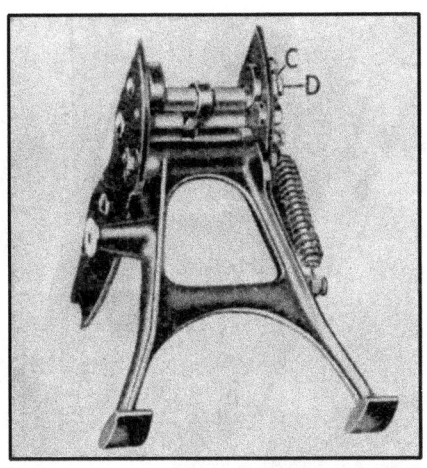

Fig. 41. Showing Primary Chain Adjustment

When the proper tension has been arrived at, tighten up the gearbox bolts, and finally, the large hexagon locking the crank. If the gearbox is tight and refuses to move, it may be advisable to slacken the chain stay bolts, which will probably free the gearbox.

To adjust the primary chain on the 250 c.c. models slacken the gearbox bolts and slide the box backwards or forwards by means of the drawbolt. This operation is made easier by also slackening the chain stay bolts. Use the smaller of the two large box spanners when tightening and slip the large one over the tommy-bar to obtain increased leverage. All these nuts must be kept very tight indeed. Adjust the gear control whenever the gearbox is moved.

Secondary Chain Adjustment. On the 250 c.c. models slacken the nut on the left side of the anchor bolt and draw the wheel backwards by means of the draw bolts, giving an equal number of turns to each side. If the wheel was correctly aligned previously, the alignment will be maintained. Finally, tighten all nuts thoroughly and readjust the rear brake control if necessary (see page 91).

On the 500 c.c. models slacken the nut on the left side of the machine and brake anchor bolt (*C*, Fig. 40). Place the spanner on the bolt head (*A*, Fig. 40) on the right side and rotate the bolt anti-clockwise to tighten. The cams on each side of the bolt will keep the wheel in perfect alignment.

To Adjust the Dynamo Chain. To tighten, loosen the strap

Fig. 42. Steering Head and Fork Adjustment

bolts and rotate the dynamo clockwise when looking at the right side.

Always replace the clip of a spring link so that its closed end faces the direction of travel.

Magneto Chain Adjustment (500 c.c.). The magneto platform is provided with adjustment and is clamped to the cradle plates by two bolts with nuts which are prevented from rotating by means of a locking plate. To adjust the table, therefore, it is necessary to slacken the bolts which can be turned by means of a spanner inserted at the rear of the oil bath chain case. The magneto can then be moved upwards and backwards by hand to give the correct chain adjustment, after which the bolt should be re-tightened. The "250's" have adjustment on right-hand side.

Avoid Play in Steering Head and Forks. Play must be taken

GARAGING AND MAINTENANCE

up if present in the steering head and forks, otherwise the steering of the machine will suffer. Occasionally, you should put the machine on its central stand, place a suitable box under the crankcase and test the steering for play by shaking the front wheel backwards and forwards. To adjust, slacken the steering damper right off, slacken locknut (*D*, Fig. 42) and tighten nut (*E*), using the *C* spanner in the tool kit. For correct adjustment the steering head should be absolutely free, yet without trace of play. Before finally testing, tighten locknut (*D*), since this may affect the adjustment. Turn the bar from side to side. If there is a tendency to remain in a central position and to resist the first few degrees of movement, the steering head races are pitted and should be replaced. If the races are pitted and the head is tightened up too much a very unpleasant sway in the steering is set up.

If the spring forks and ball head bearings are regularly lubricated with the Tecalemit greaser very little wear will take place.

To adjust the spring forks on 500 c.c. machines, slacken the locknut on the nearside of the shackle bolt, adjust by turning the shackle bolt by means of its squared end (*G*, Fig. 42) until the correct degree of adjustment is obtained, then re-tighten the locknut. An anti-clockwise rotation of the squared end of the shackle bolt slackens the adjustment and vice versa. There should be no slackness in the fork shackles, but it is vital to good steering that the forks work freely.

Gear Control Adjustment. On machines with the gear control on the tank, if the box has been moved to adjust the front chain, it is essential to check and, if necessary, correct the adjustment of the gear control rod. To adjust the control engage either second or third gears and take out the pin (*B*, Fig. 42) by removing its split pin and washer; now hold the gear lever exactly central between the shoulders of the gate. The gears themselves will be held in their correct position by the locating mechanism inside the box. Now slip the yoke end of the control rod over the end of the gear lever and see whether the pin can be inserted; if not, slacken the locknut (*A*, Fig. 42) and screw the yoke end either up or down the rod until the pin will slip into place. Tighten the locknut (*A*) and replace the washer and split pin securing the pin.

HOW TO DECARBONIZE (1933-6)

After 2,000 to 3,000 miles have been covered, the accumulation of carbon deposits on the piston crown and in various parts of the combustion chamber results in the engine losing its original "kick," and there is a marked decline in general all-round performance, accompanied by a tendency to knocking under the slightest provocation. In addition the exhaust note becomes "woolly." When this happens it is a sure indication that the time has come for undertaking a "top overhaul," or, in other words, for decarbonizing and if necessary grinding-in the valves. Carbon deposits are inevitable in internal combustion engines and are due to three things: (a) burnt lubricating oil; (b) carbonization of road dust; (c) incomplete fuel combustion. When decarbonizing it is always worth while inspecting the valve seatings and, *if necessary*, grinding-in the valves. Removal of the valves incidentally facilitates thorough cleaning of the ports.

Overhead Rocker Removal Unnecessary. There is sufficient room to remove the cylinder head without dismantling the overhead valve gear, but of course the push-rod covers and push-rods should be removed. Removal of the cylinder barrel is quite unnecessary every time the engine is decarbonized and if the engine is running fairly well it is best to remove the cylinder head only and scrape the carbon from the piston crown, top of cylinder bore, and combustion chamber. Every alternate decarbonizing, however, the barrel should come off and an inspection made of the piston and rings.

Preliminary Dismantling. Remove the carburettor and exhaust pipe or pipes. On the 500 c.c. models a set screw secures the finned clip and this screw must be loosened. Next disconnect the exhaust valve lifter cable and disconnect the H.T. lead from the B.T.-H. magneto or Lucas "Maglita" at the plug.

To Remove Cylinder Head. Slacken off the cylinder head retaining bolts by means of the special spanner supplied in the tool kit. Do not *prise* the head off, because, although this is unlikely to damage the copper washer, which is fitted between the cylinder barrel and head, it may possibly cause damage to the finning, which is rather brittle. Instead, with the *handle* of a light hammer tap the solid part of the head (not the finning) until the head is sufficiently loose to be *lifted* off.

To Remove Cylinder Barrel. Remove the barrel-retaining nuts, slackening them off diagonally and uniformly, and gently draw the barrel off with both hands. Be careful not to impose any side strain on the connecting-rod and not to let the piston skirt smack against the connecting-rod or crankcase when the barrel comes clear of the piston. Immediately the barrel is removed cover up the crankcase hole with a rag for obvious reasons.

Piston Removal. Rudge engines have fully floating gudgeon pins, and to remove the piston it is only necessary to push out the gudgeon pin. Spring circlips are not used, soft metal end caps being provided to prevent scoring of the cylinder walls. It is desirable to refit both the gudgeon-pin and piston in the same position relative to the connecting-rod as removed, and the inside of the piston should be marked to ensure this being done.

Piston Rings are Brittle. Special care should be taken when

GARAGING AND MAINTENANCE

removing piston rings because being of cast iron they are exceedingly brittle. It is unsafe to spring them out wider than the diameter of the piston crown, and the best method of removing the rings is shown in Fig. 43. Three strips of sheet tin about 1½ in. long and ⅜ in. wide are inserted under the rings opposite the slots, enabling the rings to be gently eased off one by one. Broken pieces of an old hack-saw blade will answer the same purpose.

Examine Rings. The rings should be polished round the whole of their surfaces, and if either ring is discoloured or has a black

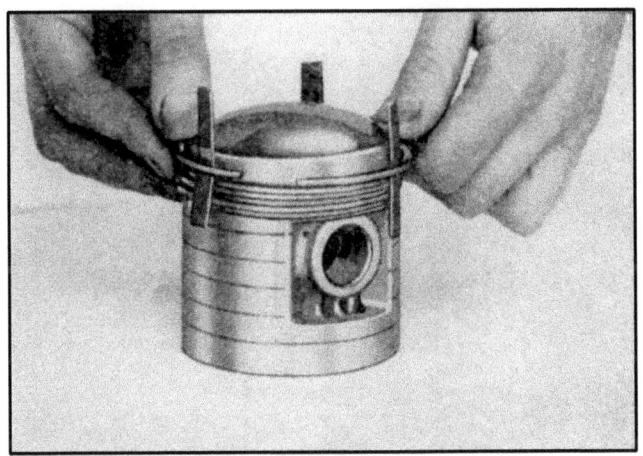

FIG. 43. A SAFE METHOD OF REMOVING PISTON RINGS
This method should also be used for replacing rings

patch on it it means that gas has been leaking past, and it should therefore be replaced by a new one. With the rings removed the piston should be washed, so that the degree of carbon deposit in the slots may be readily seen. If any is found here it should be scraped away, but extreme care is necessary in order that the surface of the slot is not damaged by the scraping tool. If it is, loss of compression will result, and if the slot is badly cut or dented a new piston will probably have to be fitted for first-class results to be obtained. Any carbon deposit on the inside of the ring should also be scraped away. It is important to note that the rings should be quite free in their grooves, without much up-and-down movement, and the gap between the ends of the ring should be 0·010 in. and 0·017 in. on the 250 c.c. Tourist and Sports engines respectively, and 0·012 in. and 0·015 in. on the "Special" and "Ulster" engines respectively.

98 THE BOOK OF THE RUDGE

Removing the Valves. All that is necessary to do this on the 500 c.c. "Special" machine is to depress the valve springs until the split collars can be removed, and the valves can then be slipped out of the cylinder head. The large closed-ended spanner can be used for depressing the springs, as shown in illustration (Fig. 44).

On the radial valve engines, however, it may be more convenient if the rocker gear is removed before the valve springs are

Fig. 44. Compressing Valve Springs on 500 c.c. "Special" Engine

depressed. This is quite a simple matter and, on the 250 c.c., Sports, and exhaust side of the "Ulster" machines, all that the reader will have to do is to remove the nuts at the top of the rocker pillars on the left-hand side of the engine, and loosen those at the pivots of the right-hand exhaust and inlet valve rockers and lever the cupped washers out of the recesses in the brackets on the right-hand side of the engine. The rocker plates and rockers can then be lifted complete from the cylinder head and the valve springs depressed in the usual way to remove the valves. If desired the rockers can then be dismantled from the plates on the bench. Care must be taken not to lose the separate contact piece from between the right- and left-hand rockers, and this should be fitted so that the longest dimension of the rectangle is horizontal.

It will facilitate the removal of the valve springs if a block of wood is put under the cylinder head to hold the valves up on their seats while the springs are being depressed. The valves should be marked to ensure their being replaced in the same positions, and if the valve springs have become weak these should be renewed. For decarbonizing, place the cylinder head lightly in a vice.

Removing the Carbon. The carbon should be removed as completely as possible; the more thoroughly this is done, the longer can be the periods between decarbonization.

All that should be necessary is to remove the carbon from the inside of the cylinder head, the piston (page 96), and the top of the cylinder bore, and this can be done by means of any fairly sharp instrument, such as a screwdriver or a penknife. Never use emery cloth for smoothing over the crown of the piston unless the cylinder barrel has been removed, as particles of emery are bound to get down on to the piston rings and result in scoring of the cylinder walls. After the carbon has been thoroughly removed from all parts, including the exhaust ports, the surfaces can be cleaned over with a calico rag damped in a little paraffin.

When cleaning the piston great care must be taken that the soft aluminium is not scratched or damaged in any way. It is inadvisable to clean the skirt of the piston, even if it has been found essential to take the piston out of the engine in order to remove the carbon from the ring grooves, and the only time the piston or cylinder walls should be smoothed at all is in the case of a slight seizure, when a dead smooth file must be used and very fine emery paper, and every trace of the abrasive must be removed before reassembling.

When removing carbon from the piston ring grooves care must be taken not to spoil their shape or enlarge them in any way. Part of an old piston ring is quite useful for this purpose. Make sure that the oil holes below the bottom ring are quite clear.

To Grind-in the Valves. First see that there are no traces of carbon left in the inside of the head and valve ports, and then thoroughly clean the valves. Smear the valve seatings lightly with grinding paste and a spot of oil and grind the valves in with the aid of a screwdriver placed in the slot in the valve head. The screwdriver should be held in the right hand and the valve turned to and fro, while the left hand should be used to lift the valve, at the end of each to and each fro movement, by pressing on the end of the valve stem. After this has been done a little time the valve can be given a quarter of a turn and the process repeated until a good seating is obtained all round. Before the valves are refitted it should be seen that they and the cylinder head are free from all traces of dirt and grinding paste and that the stems are properly lubricated.

Reassembly. This should be done in the following order—

If the piston has been removed, replace this on the connecting rod, making sure that there is plenty of oil on the gudgeon pin. When the piston rings are refitted there should be a gap between the ends of the rings, when in the cylinder bore according to the figures mentioned on page 97.

Liberally smear the outside of the piston with oil and slip the cylinder barrel over it. Paper washers should be fitted between the cylinder barrel and the crankcase or compression plate (where

Fig. 45. Showing 500 c.c. Special Cylinder Head with Exhaust Valves Dismantled

fitted) and these should be smeared with thick oil or liquid jointing material. Then replace the nuts on the studs at the cylinder base and tighten down.

The cylinder head, valves, and rocker gear should be reassembled before replacing on the engine. The valves should be replaced in the cylinder head, the springs and collars put over them and well depressed, and the split cotters slipped into place. A block of wood should be placed inside the cylinder head to hold the valves up on their seats during this process. Now reassemble the rocker gear in the reverse order from that in which it was taken down. When the cylinder head is replaced on the cylinder barrel care should be taken that the jointing surfaces are scrupulously clean and that the copper gasket washer is undamaged, and when the cylinder head holding down bolts are being screwed up these should be turned only one-sixth of a revolution each, in order, until they are all dead tight.

GARAGING AND MAINTENANCE

Finally, replace the carburettor, exhaust pipes, sparking plug and lead, and exhaust lifter cable.

Instructions for Reassembling 500 c.c. " Special " O.H. Rockers. First of all thread the inner large plate (*C*, Fig. 45) over the end of the rocker against which the push-rod bears, taking care that it is fitted so that it corresponds with the shape of the cast rocker support. Then push the rocker endwise and slide the corresponding smaller plate over the other end. Next pack the rollers (*F* and *G*) back into the races and thread the largest plate of all (*D*) over the end of the rocker adjacent to the push-rod. This should be fitted so that the sideways projection is towards the centre line of the engine, thus forming the back of the rocker casing. Now fit the split plates (*A*) to engage with the grooves in the opposite end of the rocker. These should be fitted so that they are divided horizontally. Finally, fit the convex end plate (*B*), which has a grease nipple in its centre, and bolt the plates together (*E*), finally refitting both the aluminium rocker casings. File, if necessary, the valve stems until the rocker touches both equally, and the head is ready to be refitted on the cylinder barrel as described above.

In order to refit the exhaust valve lifter the exhaust valves and overhead rocker must be depressed, and undoubtedly the best and easiest way of doing it is to insert the closed end of a thin spanner between the valve spring caps and rocker and use the latter as a fulcrum to compress the valve springs as shown in Fig. 44.

DISMANTLING RUDGE ENGINES (1933-6)

The average rider need rarely take his engine right down, and the preceding instructions should meet the maintenance requirements of most readers of this book. There are, however, some riders who for tuning, amusement or curiosity will at some time or other strip the engine "below the waist." It is for the benefit of such riders that I have included the following notes.

To Remove the Engine. If assistance is not available proceed first as for decarbonizing. If assistance is available, remove exhaust pipes, exhaust lifter control (see Fig. 38), magneto and dynamo, carburettor, H.T. lead, the oil pipes, oil bath chain case and primary and secondary chains. Then remove the bolts passing through the engine plates and lift the complete engine out and place it *safely* on the bench.

To Dismantle Shock Absorber. Slacken the nut on the end of the engine shaft and tap the washer (*A*, Fig. 46) until it is freed from its taper, when it may be removed. Remove the spring (*B*), then the splined member (*C*), and lastly the engine sprocket (*D*).

How to Dismantle Timing Gear. Both magneto chain and

sprockets (except on the 250 c.c. engines where a "Maglita" is driven at engine speed from a sprocket on the engine shaft) must be dismantled before the small bolts securing the timing cover are taken out and the cover removed. To avoid disturbing the timing, the tappets may be left in place when the cover is removed. If, for any reason, it is desirable to remove the cam wheel it will be necessary to remove the half time pinion nut and the worm from the engine shaft. The half time pinion need not be disturbed. The cam-wheel can then easily be withdrawn. If the half time pinion, however, has to be removed, a special extractor will be

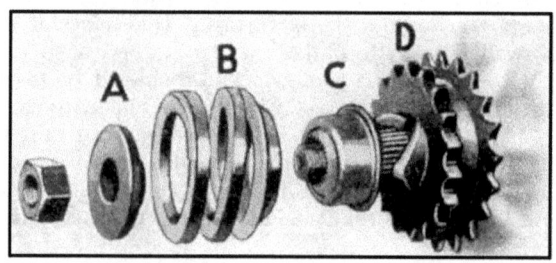

Fig 46. Component Parts of Engine Shaft Shock-Absorber

necessary to fit the threads. Before the cam-wheel is removed it is desirable to mark the meshing teeth on the cam gear and half time pinion.

Timing the Valves. If the timing has, for any reason, been disturbed, it will be necessary to set the valves carefully to open at the correct period, and this is best done as follows, with the cylinder head in place—

If the small timing pinion has been removed, push it on to its taper, together with the pump worm, making sure that the tenon on the worm engages with the slot in the pinion, but do not tighten up. Refit the cam wheel and exhaust rocker. Adjust the tappets to give a clearance of 0·02 in., except on the 250 c.c. Sports where 0·010 is required, and rotate the engine until the piston position corresponds with the timing given for the exhaust valve opening (see table opposite), the position of the piston being measured by a rod through the hole in the centre of the head. Turn the cam wheel in an anti-clockwise direction until the exhaust tappet is just tight. Now tap the worm firmly with a hammer to cause the timing pinion to bind on its taper and tighten up the nut securing the small timing pinion, check the setting to see that the pinion has not slipped while tightening, and the valves are timed—not nearly such a difficult operation as many people seem to think.

GARAGING AND MAINTENANCE

Valve Timing	250 c.c. Tourist	250 c.c. Sports	"Special"	"Ulster"
Inlet opens before T.D.C.	·2 mm.	8 mm.	·2 mm.	10·0 mm.
Inlet closes after B.D.C.	8·0 mm.	13·2 mm.	8·4 mm.	13·0 mm.
Exhaust opens before B.D.C.	13·4 mm.	13·2 mm.	14·4 mm.	16·0 mm.
Exhaust closes after T.D.C.	2·2 mm.	8 mm.	2·4 mm.	10·0 mm.

Valve Clearances. The clearances mentioned in the preceding paragraph are for timing purposes only. For running clearances and the method of setting them see page 88.

How to Re-time the Ignition. First replace the timing cover, magneto sprocket and chain, and see that one of the sprockets is

	250 c.c. Tourist	250 c.c. Sports	"Special"	"Ulster"
Magneto advance before T.D.C.	12-14 mm.	15 mm.	12-14 mm.	14-16 mm.

loose on its taper. Turn the engine over until the engine is on T.D.C. with both valves closed. Now rotate it backwards until the piston has descended according to the figures above. Set the handlebar spark lever at *full advance*, turn the magneto armature clockwise (C.B. side) until the contacts are on the point of breaking, and re-tighten the sprocket.

CLUTCH AND GEARBOX (1933-9)

To Remedy Clutch Slip. Clutch slip is unlikely (see page 57) but if it does occur, due to excessive filling of the oil bath chain case, screw up the adjustable thimbles not more than a whole turn each.

To Remove the 250 c.c. Clutch. Take off the cover plate, bend down the tang on the locking plate, undo the central nut and give the clutch a sharp blow on the front face near the edge. If this fails to loosen the clutch from its taper, an extractor should be used to fit the external threads on the central sleeve. If it should be necessary to dismantle the clutch, proceed as follows.

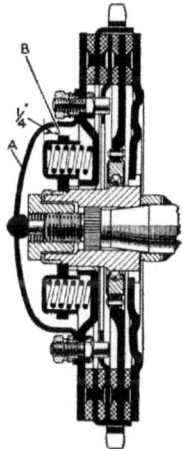

FIG. 47. THE 250 C.C. CLUTCH

First remove the cover plate (*A*, Fig. 47), unscrew the spring thimbles with screwdriver, when the central screwed ring (*B*) can be removed. The clutch plates can now be completely separated.

When reassembling see that the thin driven plate is fitted with the raised portion away from the chain sprocket, and the recessed portion of the chain sprocket away from the gear box. The spring pressure exerted is controlled by the amount the spring thimbles are screwed into the central ring and this should normally be fitted so that the ends of the thimbles stand out ¼ in. from the outer face of the ring.

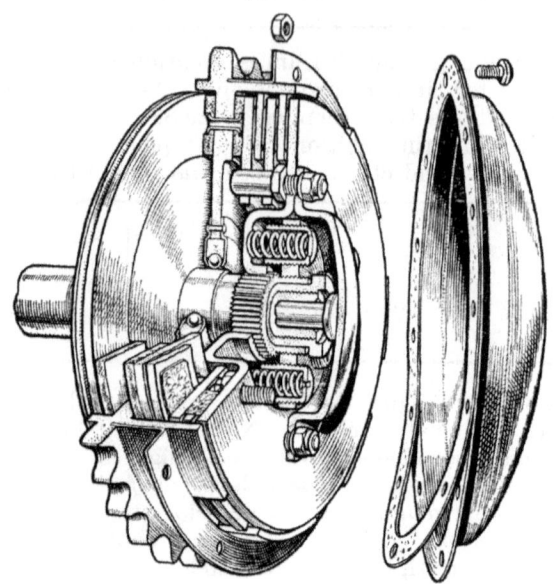

Fig. 48. The 500 c.c. Clutch with Cover Removed

On " Ulster " and Special Models the clutch is enclosed in an oil-proof case. The clutch itself has been redesigned and is of unusually sturdy proportions

To Remove 500 c.c. Clutch. To remove and dismantle the 500 c.c. clutch (see Fig. 48), proceed as for the 250 c.c. clutch, but first remove the domed cover. The correct spring pressure on this clutch is obtained when the ends of the screwed thimbles project out of the central ring by $\frac{5}{16}$ in. The sprocket for the secondary chain is held by splines and a locknut with left-hand thread.

Gearbox Overhaul.* This is really beyond the scope of most riders, and if any internal trouble occurs it is far the best plan to return the gearbox to the makers for attention. Keep the thrust rod and screw in the clutch arm lubricated.

Step-by-step Gear Change. The construction of the step-by-step mechanism is as follows: A body carries two pawls, around

* Detailed information for the overhaul of the Rudge gearbox and clutch can be found in our '1930's British Motorcycle Gearboxes & Clutches' publication

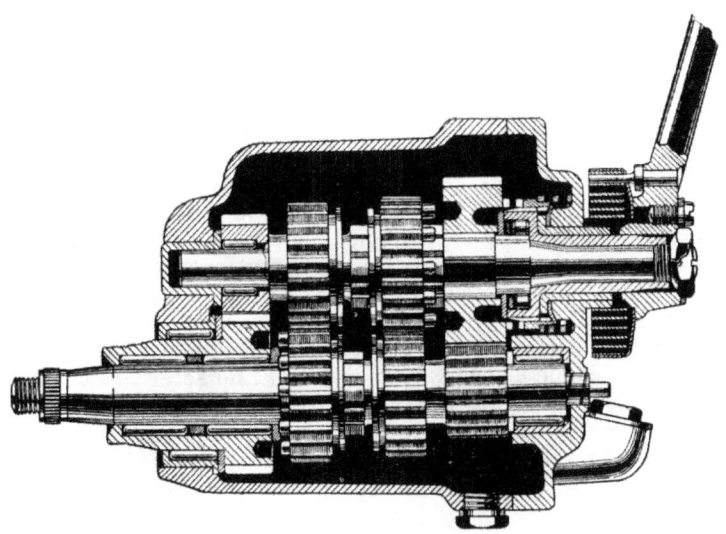

Fig. 49. Sectional View of Rudge Four-speed Gearbox

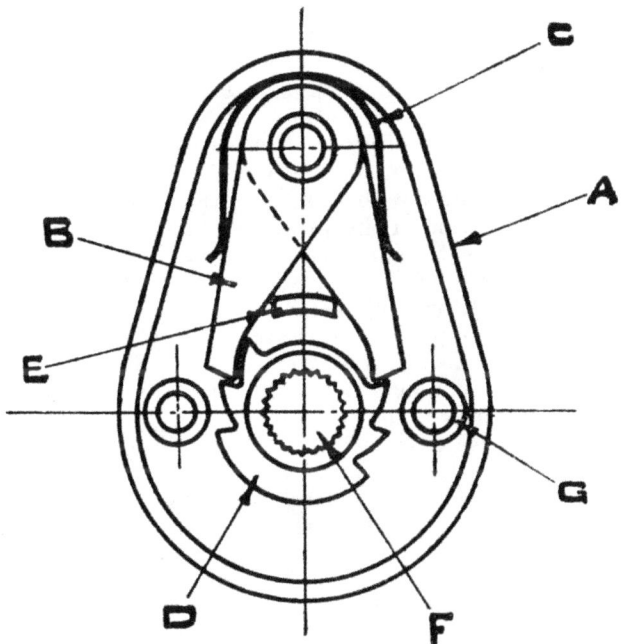

Fig. 50. Foot Gear-change Mechanism

which a leaf spring is fitted. The ends of the pawl engage ratchet teeth in a wheel and this ratchet wheel is mounted upon a gear box quadrant. The movement of the body, which is actuated by the pedal, is limited by a stop so that the quadrant can only be moved one step at a time. In the event of this mechanism being disconnected, to reassemble it is necessary that the attachment plates should first be bolted to the gearbox. Third gear should be engaged by movement of the quadrant and the ratchet wheel must be placed back on the serrations so that the wheel is in the position shown in the illustration (Fig. 50). When the correct serration is engaged the clearance between the ends of the pawls and the ratchet teeth should be approximately 0·02 in. Unless the whole gearbox is dismantled and screwed bush, which controls the position of the operating quadrant, has been altered, no difficulty should be experienced in reassembly. It will be observed that the quadrant bush has been drilled and a locking screw fitted, and this controls the position of the gears inside the box.

REMOVING ENGINE FROM FRAME (1937-9)

When the big-end or main bearings require attention, the owner is strongly urged to send his engine to the Rudge factory, or to a thoroughly qualified motor-cycle repairer.

Suitable Greases for Rudge Machines. The overhead rockers on 250 c.c. engines require to be greased, and for this purpose the following greases are suitable: Esso Grease, Price's Energrease N3, Castrolease Medium, Mobilgrease No. 2, Shell Retinax CD. The above lubricants with one exception are also suitable for grease-gun lubrication of the various cycle parts. If using Price's lubricant, the correct grade is Energrease C3. For hub lubrication use Esso Grease, Price's Energrease C3, Castrolease Heavy, Mobilgrease No. 4, or Shell R.B. Grease. Recommended greases for lubrication of exposed chains are: Esso Grease, Price's Energrease A0, Castrolease G, Mobilgrease No. 2, Shell Retinax CD.

Assuming the cylinder head is already removed and the magneto drive dismantled, the procedure is as follows: Take off the primary chain case cover. Slacken back the nut on the driving shaft two or three threads and tap the large washer *A* (Fig. 46) until it loosens on its taper and contacts with the nut again. Remove the nut and withdraw the shock absorber parts from the shaft. Remove the clutch cover, undo the central lock-nut, when, by lightly tapping the back of the clutch, the latter, together with the primary chain and drawing sprocket, may be withdrawn from the case. The dynamo sprocket must be taken off when removal of the chain case and engine from the frame are self evident.

INDEX

ACCIDENTS, 26, 28
Amal carburettor, 42
—— ——, tuning, 75
Avon tyre pressures, 72

BATTERY, care of, 85
—— charging, 86
Braking system, 57, 91
B.T.-H. magneto generator, 48, 79

CARBON, removing, 99
Carburettor, action of, 40
——, tuning, 74
Clutch adjustment, 90
—— lubrication, 51
—— removal, 103
—— slip, 103
Contact-breaker, 79
Controls, 13
Cylinder, removing, 64, 96

DANGEROUS driving, 28
Decarbonizing, 62, 95
Depreciation, 8
Dismantling engine, 67, 101
Driving, 13
—— licence, 3, 28
—— tests, 31
Dry-sump lubrication system, 39
Dynamo, 83
—— chain, adjusting, 94
—— lubrication, 48

ENGINE lubrication, 45
——, working of, 32
Exhaust valve lifter adjustment, 90

FILTERS, cleaning, 47
Focusing head lamp, 87
Four-stroke cycle, 34

GARAGING, 53
Gearbox lubrication, 49

Gearbox, Rudge, 105
Grinding-in the valves, 99

HYDROMETER, 86

IGNITION maintenance, 73
Insurance, 3, 29
Interchangeable wheels, 60

JET, carburettor, 76

LUBRICATION, 44, 106
Lucas "Maglita," 48, 80

MAGNETO lubrication, 48
—— maintenance, 79
Miller dynamo, 83

OIL bath chain case, 49, 52
—— circulation, 47
—— pump, 39, 48
Oils, engine, 44

PEDESTRIAN crossings, 31
Physical fitness, 30
Pillion riding, 21, 30
Piston removal, 64, 96
—— rings, 97
Polarity, dynamo, reversed, 83
Primary chain adjustment, 92

RADIAL valve head, 38
Registration licences, 2
Road sense, 15
—— traffic Act, 28
Rocker lubrication, overhead, 48, 106
Running costs, 8

SECONDARY chain adjustment, 93
—— —— lubrication, 50
Second-hand, buying, 5
——, selling, 11
Sidecar alignment, 70
Silence, 18, 31

Skidding, 20
Sparking plug, 78
Speed limit, 31
Steering head adjustment, 62, 95
—— —— lubrication, 51

TAPPETS, adjusting, 88
Taxation, 1
Timing, ignition, 69, 103
——, valve, 68, 102
Touring, 10
Transmission, lubrication, 50

Twist-grip adjustment, 90
Tyre pressures, 71
—— removal, 73

VALVE clearances, 54, 87
Valves, removing, 98

WHEEL alignment, 69
—— bearings, adjusting, 91
Wheels, lubrication of, 51, 106
——, removing, 59, 92
Wiring diagrams, 82, 84

AUTOBOOKS WORKSHOP MANUALS

ALFA ROMEO GIULIA 1300, 1600, 1750, 2000 1962-1978 WSM
BMW 1600 1966-1973 WSM
BMW 2500, 2800, 3.0 & 3.3 1968-1977 WSM
BMW 316, 320, 320i 1975-1977 WSM
BMW 518, 520, 520i 1973-1981 WSM
FIAT 1100, 1100D, 1100R & 1200 1957-1969 WSM
FIAT 124 1966-1974 WSM
FIAT 124 SPORT 1966-1975 WSM
FIAT 125 & 125 SPECIAL 1967-1973 WSM
FIAT 126, 126L, 126 DV, 126/650 & 126/650 DV 1972-1982 WSM
FIAT 127 SALOON, SPECIAL & SPORT, 900, 1050 1971-1981 WSM
FIAT 128 1969-1982 WSM
FIAT 1300, 1500 1961-1967 WSM
FIAT 131 MIRAFIORI 1975-1982 WSM
FIAT 132 1972-1982 WSM
FIAT 500 1957-1973 WSM
FIAT 600, 600D & MULTIPLA 1955-1969 WSM
FIAT 850 1964-1972 WSM
JAGUAR MK 1, 2 1955-1969 WSM
JAGUAR S TYPE, 420 1963-1968 WSM
JAGUAR XK 120, 140, 150 MK 7, 8, 9 1948-1961 WSM
LAND ROVER 1, 2 1948-1961 WSM
MERCEDES-BENZ 190 1959-1968 WSM
MERCEDES-BENZ 220/8 1968-1972 WSM
MERCEDES-BENZ 220B 1959-1965 WSM
MERCEDES-BENZ 230 1963-1968 WSM
MERCEDES-BENZ 250 1968-1972 WSM
MERCEDES-BENZ 280 1968-1972 WSM
MINI 1959-1980 WSM
MORRIS MINOR 1952-1971 WSM
PEUGEOT 404 1960-1975 WSM
PORSCHE 911 1964-1973 WSM
PORSCHE 911 1970-1977 WSM
RENAULT 16 1965-1979 WSM
RENAULT 8, 10, 1100 1962-1971 WSM
ROVER 3500, 3500S 1968-1976 WSM
SUNBEAM RAPIER, ALPINE 1955-1965 WSM
TRIUMPH SPITFIRE, GT6, VITESSE 1962-1968 WSM
TRIUMPH TR4, TR4A 1961-1967 WSM
VOLKSWAGEN BEETLE 1968-1977 WSM

VELOCEPRESS AUTOMOBILE BOOKS & MANUALS

ABARTH BUYERS GUIDE
AUSTIN-HEALEY 6-CYLINDER WSM
AUSTIN-HEALEY SPRITE & MG MIDGET 1958-1971 WSM
BMW 600 LIMOUSINE FACTORY WSM
BMW 600 LIMOUSINE OWNERS HAND BOOK & SERVICE MANUAL
BMW 2000 & 2002 1966-1976 WSM
BMW ISETTA FACTORY WSM
BOOK OF THE CARRERA PANAMERICANA - MEXICAN ROAD RACE
COMPLETE CATALOG OF JAPANESE MOTOR VEHICLES
CORVAIR 1960-1969 OWNERS WORKSHOP MANUAL
CORVETTE V8 1955-1962 OWNERS WORKSHOP MANUAL
DIALED IN - THE JAN OPPERMAN STORY
FERRARI 250/GT SERVICE AND MAINTENANCE
FERRARI 308 SERIES BUYER'S AND OWNER'S GUIDE
FERRARI BERLINETTA LUSSO
FERRARI BROCHURES AND SALES LITERATURE 1946-1967
FERRARI BROCHURES AND SALES LITERATURE 1968-1989
FERRARI GUIDE TO PERFORMANCE
FERRARI OPP, MAINTENANCE & SERVICE H/BOOKS 1948-1963
FERRARI OWNER'S HANDBOOK
FERRARI SERIAL NUMBERS PART I - ODD NUMBERS TO 21399
FERRARI SERIAL NUMBERS PART II - EVEN NUMBERS TO 1050
FERRARI SPYDER CALIFORNIA
FERRARI TUNING TIPS & MAINTENANCE TECHNIQUES
HENRY'S FABULOUS MODEL "A" FORD
HOW TO BUILD A FIBERGLASS CAR
HOW TO BUILD A RACING CAR
HOW TO RESTORE THE MODEL 'A' FORD
IF HEMINGWAY HAD WRITTEN A RACING NOVEL
JAGUAR E-TYPE 3.8 & 4.2 WSM
LE MANS 24 (THE BOOK THAT THE FILM WAS BASED ON)
MASERATI BROCHURES AND SALES LITERATURE
MASERATI OWNER'S HANDBOOK
METROPOLITAN FACTORY WSM
MGA & MGB OWNERS HANDBOOK & WSM
MG MIDGET TC, TD, TF & TF1500 WORKSHOP MANUAL
OBERT'S FIAT GUIDE
PERFORMANCE TUNING THE SUNBEAM TIGER
PORSCHE 356 1948-1965 WSM
PORSCHE 912 WSM
SOUPING THE VOLKSWAGEN
SOLEX CARBURETORS (EMPHASIS ON UK & EU AUTOMOBILES)
SU CARBURETORS (EMPHASIS ON UK AUTOMOBILES)
TRIUMPH TR2, TR3, TR4 1953-1965 WSM
TUNING FOR SPEED (P.E. IRVING)
VEDA ORR'S NEW REVISED HOT ROD PICTORIAL
VOLKSWAGEN TRANSPORTER, TRUCKS, STATION WAGONS WSM
VOLVO 1944-1968 ALL MODELS WSM
WEBER CARBURETORS (EMPHASIS ON ALFA & FIAT)

BROOKLANDS BOOKS & ROAD TEST PORTFOLIOS (RTP)

AC CARS 1904-2009
ALFA ROMEO 1920-1933 ROAD TEST PORTFOLIO
ALFA ROMEO 1934-1940 ROAD TEST PORTFOLIO
BRABHAM RALT HONDA THE RON TAURANAC STORY
BUGATTI TYPE 10 TO TYPE 40 ROAD TEST PORTFOLIO
BUGATTI TYPE 10 TO TYPE 251 ROAD TEST PORTFOLIO
BUGATTI TYPE 41 TO TYPE 55 ROAD TEST PORTFOLIO
BUGATTI TYPE 57 TO TYPE 251 ROAD TEST PORTFOLIO
DELAHAYE ROAD TEST PORTFOLIO
FERRARI ROAD CARS 1946-1956 ROAD TEST PORTFOLIO
FIAT 500 1936-1972 ROAD TEST PORTFOLIO
FIAT DINO ROAD TEST PORTFOLIO
HISPANO SUIZA ROAD TEST PORTFOLIO
HONDA ST1100/ST1300 PAN EUROPEAN 1990-2002 RTP
JAGUAR MK1 & MK2 ROAD TEST PORTFOLIO
LOTUS CORTINA ROAD TEST PORTFOLIO
MV AGUSTA F4 750 & 1000 1997-2007 ROAD TEST PORTFOLIO
TATRA CARS ROAD TEST PORTFOLIO

VELOCEPRESS MOTORCYCLE BOOKS & MANUALS

1930'S BRITISH MOTORCYCLE GEARBOXES & CLUTCHES (BOOK OF)
AJS SINGLES & TWINS 250cc THRU 1000cc 1932-1948 (BOOK OF)
AJS SINGLES 1955-65 350cc & 500cc (BOOK OF)
AJS SINGLES 1945-60 350cc & 500cc MODELS 16 & 18 (BOOK OF)
ARIEL 1939-1960 4 STROKE SINGLES (BOOK OF)
ARIEL LEADER & ARROW 1958-1964 (BOOK OF)
ARIEL MOTORCYCLES 1933-1951 WSM
ARIEL PREWAR MODELS 1932-1939 (BOOK OF)
BMW M/CYCLES R26 R27 (1956-1967) FACTORY WSM
BMW M/CYCLES R50 R50S R60 R69S (1955-1969) FACTORY WSM
BSA BANTAM ALL MODELS FROM 1948 ONWARDS (BOOK OF)
BSA SINGLES & V-TWINS UP TO 1927 (BOOK OF)
BSA SINGLES & V-TWINS 1936-1939 (BOOK OF)
BSA SINGLES & V-TWINS 1936-1952 (BOOK OF)
BSA OHV & SV SINGLES 250-600cc 1945-1954 (BOOK OF)
BSA OHV & SV SINGLES - 250cc 1954-1970 (BOOK OF)
BSA OHV SINGLES 350 & 500cc 1955-1967 (BOOK OF)
BSA TWINS 1948-1962 (BOOK OF)
BSA TWINS 1962-1969 (SECOND BOOK OF)
CATALOG OF BRITISH MOTORCYCLES (1951 MODELS)
DOUGLAS PRE-WAR ALL MODELS 1929-1939 (BOOK OF)
DOUGLAS POST-WAR ALL MODELS 1948-1957 FACTORY WSM
DUCATI 160cc, 250cc & 350cc OHC MODELS FACTORY WSM
HONDA 50 ALL MODELS UP TO 1970 INC MONKEY & TRAIL (BOOK OF)
HONDA 90 ALL MODELS UP TO 1966 (BOOK OF)
HONDA MOTORCYCLES 125-150 TWINS C/CS/CB/CA WSM
HONDA MOTORCYCLES 250-305 TWINS C/CS/CB WSM
HONDA MOTORCYCLES C100 SUPER CUB WSM
HONDA MOTORCYCLES C110 SPORT CUB 1962-1969 WSM
HONDA TWINS & SINGLES 50cc THRU 305cc 1960-1966 (BOOK OF)
HONDA TWINS ALL MODELS 125cc THRU 450cc UP TO 1968 (BOOK OF)
INDIAN PONYBIKE, BOY RACER & PAPOOSE ILL PARTS LIST & SALES LIT
J.A.P. ENGINES 1927-1952 & MOTORCYCLES 1934-1952 (BOOK OF)
LAMBRETTA ALL MODELS 1947-1957 (BOOK OF)
LAMBRETTA LI & TV MODELS 1957-1970 (SECOND BOOK OF)
MATCHLESS 350 & 500cc SINGLES 1945-1956 (BOOK OF)
MATCHLESS 350 & 500cc SINGLES 1955-1966 (BOOK OF)
MOTORCYCLE ENGINEERING (P. E. Irving)
NORTON 1932-1947 (BOOK OF)
NORTON 1938-1956 (BOOK OF)
NORTON DOMINATOR TWINS 1955-1965 (BOOK OF)
NORTON MODELS 19, 50 & ES2 1955-1963 (BOOK OF)
NORTON MOTORCYCLES 1957-1970 FACTORY WSM
NORTON PREWAR MODELS 1932-1939 (BOOK OF)
NSU PRIMA ALL MODELS 1956-1964 (BOOK OF)
NSU QUICKLY ALL MODELS 1953-1963 (BOOK OF)
RALEIGH MOPEDS 1960-1969 (BOOK OF)
RALEIGH MOTORCYCLES 1919-1933 (BOOK OF)
ROYAL ENFIELD SINGLES & V TWINS 1934-1946 (BOOK OF)
ROYAL ENFIELD SINGLES & V TWINS 1937-1953 (BOOK OF)
ROYAL ENFIELD SINGLES 1946-1962 (BOOK OF)
ROYAL ENFIELD 736cc INTERCEPTOR FACTORY WSM
ROYAL ENFIELD 250cc & 350cc SINGLES 1958-1966 (SECOND BOOK OF)
RUDGE MOTORCYCLES 1933-1939 (BOOK OF)
SPEED AND HOW TO OBTAIN IT
SUNBEAM MOTORCYCLES 1928-1939 (BOOK OF)
SUNBEAM S7 & S8 1946-1957 (BOOK OF)
SUZUKI 50cc & 80cc UP TO 1966 (BOOK OF)
SUZUKI T10 1963-1967 FACTORY WSM
SUZUKI T20 & T200 1965-1969 FACTORY WSM
TRIUMPH PRE-WAR MOTORCYCLE 1935-1939 (BOOK OF)
TRIUMPH MOTORCYCLES 1935-1949 (BOOK OF)
TRIUMPH MOTORCYCLES 1937-1951 WSM
TRIUMPH MOTORCYCLES 1945-1955 FACTORY WSM
TRIUMPH TWINS 1945-1958 (BOOK OF)
TRIUMPH TWINS 1956-1969 (BOOK OF)
VELOCETTE ALL SINGLES & TWINS 1925-1970 (BOOK OF)
VESPA 1951-1961 (BOOK OF)
VESPA 125 & 150cc & GS MODELS 1955-1963 (SECOND BOOK OF)
VESPA 90, 125 & 150cc 1963-1972 (THIRD BOOK OF)
VESPA GS & SS 1955-1968 (BOOK OF)
VILLIERS ENGINE (BOOK OF)
VINCENT MOTORCYCLES 1935-1955 WSM

Please check our website:

www.VelocePress.com

for a complete up-to-date list of available titles

www.ingramcontent.com/pod-product-compliance
Lightning Source LLC
Chambersburg PA
CBHW070557170426
43201CB00012B/1870